THE EWE OF GHANA AND TOGO ON THE EVE OF COLONIALISM

(A Contribution to the Marxist Debate on pre-capitalist Socio-economic Formations)

ANSA K. ASAMOA

 GHANA PUBLISHING CORPORATION

First Published 1986 by the
Publishing Division of the
Ghana Publishing Corporation
Private Mail Bag, Tema, Ghana

ISBN 9964 1 0298 4

Printed by the
Tema Press of the
Ghana Publishing Corporation

To Barbara, Sayi, Tatjana, and Mathias

ACKNOWLEDGEMENT

I thank Prof. Francis Agbodeka and Associate Prof. Kofi Awoonor, former Heads of the History and English Departments, respectively of the University of Cape Coast, as well as Associate Prof. D. Amenumey, of the Department of History of the same University, for their assessment of the manuscript of this essay.

My thanks also go to Prof. Akilagpa Sawyerr, Vice-Chancellor of the University of Ghana and Dr. Kwesi Botchwey, formerly a Senior Lecturer at the Law Faculty of the University of Ghana and now Secretary for Finance and Economic Planning of Ghana, for their critical observations.

Mr. Atta Britwum, a Senior Lecturer and former Head of the French Department of the University of Cape Coast, Prof. O. Onogo, Head of the Sociology Department of the University of Jos, Prof. G. Hauck, formerly of the University of Heidelberg, Mr. Yao Graham, a former Lecturer at the Law Faculty of the University of Ghana and Dr. L. K. Agbosu of University of Benin have rigorously discussed the manuscript with me on different occasions. I owe them special thanks.

My gratitude finally goes to Togbe Agokoli III, the present political ruler of Notsie (Togo) and his elders for the useful data they put at my disposal during my short stay in Notsie in December 1976.

A. A.

CONTENTS

CONTENTS

INTRODUCTION

The historical studies of the Ewe of Ghana and Togo have hitherto paid little attention to the economic aspect of social change the Ewe have been going through. I draw attention to this problem in my book[1] which came out in 1971.

In that book I emphasize the role of economic relations in the process of social change among the Ewe people since colonialism. I am unable to examine the pre-colonial period in detail in that study due to lack of data. But over the past two years I have managed to collect interesting data through interviews. The field information gathered, in addition to documentary material collected earlier in both German Democratic Republic and Federal Republic of Germany, serve as a fairly reliable guide in the present study.

My main concern has been to periodize, that is to say, to identify the major phases of pre-colonial Ewe social history in terms of socio-economic formation.

The rationale behind this exercise is manifold:
1. The exercise will cast more light not only on the thesis pursued in my earlier book but also on the process of state development among the Ewe in the pre-colonial time.
2. The exercise may give students of Ewe-Adja-Yoruba History a deeper historical, materialist insight into historical categories metaphysically simplified, if not vulgarized, by bourgeois historians.
3. By discussing sensitive aspects of Karl Marx's concept of *Asiatic Mode of Production* in relation to the Ewe historical experience the study challenges those social scientists, both Marxist and non-Marxist, who attach the feudal label to non-feudal traditional African societies.

This third point is of special interest, because of tactical and strategic blunders caused by Marxists as a result of their inability to correctly assess the essence of rural production relations in developing countries.

We are guided in the pursuit of these objectives by the Marxist concept of state, a concept which, though clearly defined, is still misunderstood, and consequently wrongly applied by social scientists including Marxists. One source of this confusion is Marx's use of the term, "state" in his examination of pre-capitalist class'ess societies in the *Grundrisse* (see *Grundrisse*, pp. 474–475). We are not sure why Marx depicts the classical ancient commune as a state though he himself writes, "Property, then, originally

[1] Asamoa, A., 1971.

means—in its Asiatic, Slavonic, ancient, classical, Germanic form —the relation of the working (producing or self-reproducing) subject to the conditions of his production or reproduction as his own. It will therefore have different forms depending on the condition of this production. Production itself aims at the reproduction of the producer within and together with these, his objective conditions of existence. This relation as proprietor — not as a result but as a presupposition of labour, i.e. of production — presupposes the individual defined as a member of a clan or community (whose property the individual himself is, up to a certain point) " (*Grundrisse*, p. 495). A closer study of the text, however, seems to suggest that Marx uses the term, state, here only in terms of a politically organized territorial entity (and not as an organ of coercion) committed not only to safeguarding the harmony between its forces and relations of production, but also to the defence and protection of all its members against aggression from outside. He writes, for example: "The commune —as state—is, on one side, the relation of these free and equal private proprietors to one another, their bond against the outside, and at the same time their safeguard."[2]

In spite of this difficulty Marx and Engels consistently regard the state as an organ of repression which is socially conditioned and therefore historically transient, as a social phenomenon whose evolvement is rooted in the process of class formation. Their concept of state development could be simplified as follows: The development of the state is closely linked with the development of forces of production. The more developed the forces of production, the higher the productivity of labour becomes. High labour productivity generates surplus production; surplus production ushers in social division of labour which in turn gives birth to social classes.[3] But social classes are not equal materially and socially. Some are privileged while others are under-privileged. In order to protect their economic and social privileges in society against other classes which very often constitute the majority of the population, the privileged minority develops superstructural organs of coercion, by means of which they keep the status quo.

These organs of coercion (army and police, legal system and parliament, judiciary, civil service) constitute state power. Marx/ Engels point out that it is the economically privileged classes which also wield political power. The state as an instrument of oppression can endo-geneously develop without external influence. It could also be imposed by a foreign power with a state tradition on a stateless community.

The state does not suddenly appear. As pointed out earlier it undergoes long historical processes. Whenever contradictions begin

---

[2] Marx, K. *Grundrisse*, 1977, p. 475.
[3] Social division of labour implies, among other things, the individualization of the products of labour and means of production and therefore of property. Quantitative and qualitative difference in property or wealth accumulation gives rise to social inequality and stratification.

to emerge between the forces and relations of production in a classless primitive community, the embryo of classes (and, therefore, of the state) develops. The late of state development is therefore determined by the rate of private acquisition of property. Primitive superstructural institutions such as primitive law, gerontocratic authority enjoyed by elders' councils, tributes, organized warriors, administrative nobility, which constitute the repository of political power in classless and semi-class societies, are, in actual fact, rudiments of emerging state power.[4] Engels points out that these primitive organs of coercion are usually insignificant in terms of oppression because of the undeveloped class contradictions within the social set-up.[5] The state is fully developed where classes are mature. In other words, the peaceful development of the state in primitive communities assumes repressive and aggressive character the more wealth becomes concentrated in the hands of the minority in society.

Parts I and II of the essay examine briefly and descriptively the social and economic structure of the Pre-colonial Ewe in a diachronic perspective, with special emphasis on qualitative changes taking place in the system of production relations.

It is interesting to note that the Ewe rural communities today in Ghana and Togo still maintain largely external properties of pre-colonial socio-economic relations in spite of the rapid process of disintegration of the traditional social system in favour of the dominant capitalist mode of production.[6] The pre-colonial beginning of the disintegration process is treated in detail in parts II and III.

Part III, the most important part of the work, is partly a theoretical abstraction of the concrete data descriptively arranged in parts I and II. The theoretical considerations, however, relate to works of Marx/Engels on primitive communities.

I am aware of the debate the use of terms like *savagery, barbarism* and *primitive* has been generating among anthropologists and other social scientists. As will be seen in Part III of the essay Morgan and Engels use *savagery* and *barbarism* to denote specific modes of production. Efforts to substitute terms like *communalist, precapitalist or tributory, ancient* modes of production for them are still being debated.

In analysing the Ewe Social historical experience the terms *communalism* and *palaeo-Communalism* are substituted for *Barbarism* and *Savagery* (all the three stages of Savagery) respectively. *Early, Meso,* and *Late Stages of Communalism* are used in place of *Lower, Middle* and *Upper Stages of Barbarism.*

In my view the terms *Palaeo-Communalist* and *Communalist* modes of production portray better the essence of the "Savage" and

---

4 See *Engels, F.,* 1969, p. 14 (*Anti-Duehring*)
5 For more information on the state see Engels, F., *Anti-Duehring; The Origin . . .; The German ideology*; Marx, K., *Capital I*;
6 See *Asamoa, A.,* 1971.

"Barbarian" socio-economic relations discussed by F. Engels in *The Origin of the Family, Private Property and the State.*

In other words, palaeo-Communalist and Communalist socio-economic relations are essentially identical with savage and barbarian modes of production respectively.

It is posited implicity in course of the theoretical discussions in Part III that the *Barbarian* and the *Asiatic Modes of Production* are qualitatively the same, a notion which implies that the term communalist mode of production can also be substituted for *Asiatic Mode of Production.*

Communalism is to be understood as a pre-industrial social order (with or without rudimentary class development) in which economic and political power is wielded largely by the mass of the people as expressed:

(a) in the people's collective control and democratic use of the most important means of production including land;
(b) in democratic distribution of products of labour and social facilities; and
(c) in the involvement of all the people in taking major political and administrative decisions.

Because of its dynamic nature communalist mode of production generates internal contradictions at certain stages of its development which finally lead to its negation by a qualitatively higher form of social order.

It is necessary to emphasize one vital point, namely, that it is not my intention to find a solution to the well known, very often, unnecessary, controversial debate on the concept of *Asiatic Mode of Production.* But I would wish to warn that I am not in any way impressed by the rather misleading argument that the *Marxian concept* of the AMP should be discarded because private ownership of land has allegedly dominated production relations in Asia (notably in Java, India, Sri Lanka, etc.) from time immemorial,[7] and secondly because of the peculiar geographic specification of the concept which allegedly implies the non-existence of similar modes of production outside Asia.

Karl Marx was not unaware of the fact that private property in land had existed in parts of pre-colonial Asia. In a letter he wrote to Engels on June 14, 1853, discussing a publication by Carey, an American economist, Marx writes, "As to the question of property, this is a very controversial one among the English writers on India. In the broken hill country, South of Krishna, property in land does seem to have existed. In Java, on the other hand, Sir Stamford Raffles, former English Governor of Java, observes, ". . . the sovereign was absolute landlord of the whole surface of the land where rent to any considerable amount was attainable . . ."[8] . . .

---

[7] See Wertheim, W., 1974, Ch. I.
[8] Marx, K., *Moscow* 1965, p. 86 (Karl Marx and Frederick Engels, *Selected correspondence*).

It was 4–5 years later that Marx developed the concept of Asiatic Mode of Production (*Grundrisse*).

In spite of his awareness of the existence of private property in land in parts of Asia, Marx apparently was under the impression that communal ownership of land had been dominant in Asia till colonial rule.[9]

Even if it is true, as Marx's critics claim, that recent research results indicate that it was rather private property in land which dominated production, the AMP concept could still be said to reflect historical reality in parts of Asia.

A lot of travellers' accounts and anthropological writings of late 19th Century and the 20th Century (by scholars like L. Rollin, E. Best, A. S. Thomson, To Rangi Hiroa, W. Ellis, E. G. Burrow, R. Firth, E. S. Handy, etc.) clearly show that the pre-colonial societies of several islands of the South Seas fall conveniently into the category of *Asiatic Mode of Production*. The same could be said of a large number of communities such as the so-called Paleo-Asians and peasant groups on the mainland as the works and reports of people like Atlasow, Steller, Kraschjmikow, Tolemeu, Ley Diakonos, Thietmas and many other scholars and travellers, show.

It is mere petty-bourgeois pedantry to argue that the AMP concept could not be applied universally because of its alleged geographic specification. In my opinion, there is nothing wrong with depicting an African or South American polity an *Asiatic Mode of Production* if the essence of the production relations of that society qualitatively reflects the AMP concept because the most important category being used as criterion of qualitative identification is not the geographic position of the polity but rather its true production relations.

Lack of adequate historical data renders certain theoretical conclusions in the work vulnerable to criticism. While this weakness is unfortunate we should not underrate the weight of some of the scanty data in terms of our theoretical deductions. It is hoped that loopholes in the essay would rather generate more research interests for the topic under discussion.

---

[9] See (a) *Engels to Marx*, (June 6, 1853).
　　(b) *Marx to Engels*, (June 14, 1853).
　In: *Karl Marx and Frederick Engels, Selected correspondence*, Moscow, 1953, pp. 82–86.

PART 1

LOCATION AND ENVIRONMENT

The Ewe inhabit south-eastern Ghana and southern parts of the Republics of Togo and Benin.[1] Bounded by the Atlantic Ocean in the south, the home territory of the Ewe stretches up to latitude 8°N. The easterly neighbours of the Ewe (in south-eastern Ghana and southern Togo) are the Fon who are still regarded as part of the Ewe-stock. Both groups are separated from each other by River Mono. Forming the western boundary, the Volta separates the Ewe from the Ga-Adangbe, Ga and the Akan. The territory is bounded in the north by the Akposo, the Kebu, Boasu and Buem.

Three main different physical areas characterize the region, namely the Coastal Strip, the Central Plains and the Highlands. Stretching from the Mono estuary (in the east) to the Volta estuary (in the West) the Coastal Strip covers a 5—12-kilometer-wide sand-bank and has the so-called Accra-Togoland Dry, Coastal Climate. Three large lagoons (the Keta Lagoon, Togo Lagoon and the Anexo Lagoon) separate the sand strip from the Central Plains.

In spite of the low rainfall in the area (about 532 mm yearly) the coastal sand strip is the most densely populated area in Ewe-land. Important commercial towns and cities, such as Keta, Lome, Anexo, Denu, Aflao are situated on the sand-bank. The rich, natural resources in the coastal areas contribute greatly to the high population density in the area. The sea, the lagoons and the fertile plots of sandy land near them make the development of a complex economy—fishing, salt industry, agriculture, trade—possible. Intensive cultivation of maize, manioc, onion and coconut is lucrative on the coast.

The Central Plains spread out about 240 kilometers upland in the East but do not reach beyond 40—45 kilometers in the West. Their breadth (from the Mono river to the Volta) is 190—200 kilometers.

The vegetation in the Central Plains is wet savanna. Savanna woodland with widely spaced short trees; a more or less continuous carpet of grass; baobab, fan and oil palms mainly constitute the flora. Food crops characteristic of the Central Plains are different species of yam (dioscorea alata), maize (zea mays), banana and plantain (musa paradisiaca, musa sapientum), groundnut (arachis hypogaea), beans (phaseolus vulgaris), etc. Further up-country, the vegetation becomes richer especially in the vicinities

[1] The Geographical data are based on Spieth J., 1906; Manshard W., 1961; Boateng E, 1959; Asamoa A., 1971. Note that in this discussion we are mainly concerned with the Ewe in Ghana and Togo.

1

of the rivers Todzie, Haho and Tsawe. The banks of these rivers are clothed in thick deciduous forests, while stretches of land not far away from them and other rivers and brooks are covered with gallery forests. The southern skirt of the Central Plains lies outside the wet savanna zone and is therefore dry, a situation which makes life difficult during the dry season.

Climatically the Central Plains are under the influence of the semi-seasonal Equatorial Climate with the average rainfall in the area varying from 810 mm with 73 rainy days to 1270 mm with 100 rainy days.[2] The population density in the Central Plains is very low because of constant water shortage that characterizes the area. At the beginning of the 20th Century there were only 17 settlements *(Duwo)* there while the Coastal Strip was congested with 50.[3] Population density increases gradually from south-west to north-east.

Interrupted by the Volta in the South, i.e. in the Akwamu area, the Ewe Mountain Ranges meet near Avatime forming the Kpoeta-Agome Massif. Branching off towards Agome the Kpoeta-Agome Massif finally develops into mountain chains such as the Logba and Leklebi mountains. There are many valleys in this particular area. The Agome Mountain Range spreads out northwards as far as Akposo and Danyi; the Akposo Mountain Chain proceeds further northwards till it merges with the Atakpame Mountain Range. S.tuated on the westerly side of the Ewe Moun'ains are the Santrokofi-Akpafu and Buem mountains running northwards from the Danyi mountains up to Adele. The heights of these mountains range from 500–1000 m. The monotony of the Central Plains is interrupted by the detached Adaklu and Agu mountains, as well as the Taviefe-Dodome mountains.

Covered with forests, several valleys and mountain slopes in the highland areas are fertile; grass, however dominates the vegetation on higher locations. The yearly average rainfall (1397–1788 mm) is periodically and spatially well distributed. The fertility of soil in this wet savanna area, the gallery forests, the countless rivulets, streams and fountains available—all favour lucrative cultivation of food crops and a cash crop economy. The population density in the hilly areas is high.

Historical Background

Scholars of Ewe History and Culture have depended largely on oral traditions, a situation which explains partly why their attempts at reconstructing the historical past of the Ewe leave much to be desired. In spite of this deficiency their contributions depict important episodes and events in the socio-historical past of the Ewe people, which could be very useful in any genuine attempt at historical reconstruction.

[2] Spieth. J., 1906, p. 12.
[3] *Op. Cit.,* p. 677

2

Genesis

According to available sources the cradle of the Ewe is Ketu in the south eastern part of the Republic of Benin (formerly Dahomey).[4] Westermann claims that the Ewe, Ga-Adangbe, the Yoruba and the Fon of Dahomey once lived together in Ketu which was a city state and political sub-unit of the powerful Oyo Empire.[5] There are scarcely any archaelogical material and historical documents on Ketu's early political development. Parrinder attributes the founding of the Ketu city polity to a king called Ede from Ife. This implies that Ketu's history began with monarchical rule. Parrinder claims that the 48th king of Ketu was installed in 1937. If we accept his suggestion that on the average about 5 kings ruled Ketu in a century[6] it would mean that about 47 kings ruled for 940 years, in which case the Ketu city polity must be 960 years old in the 20th year of the reign of the 48th king. Now Parrinder's *The story of Ketu* was published in 1956, i.e. the 19th year of the rule of the 48th king of Ketu.[7] If we subtract 960 years from 1956 years we get 996. We could then on the basis of this calculation conclude that the Ketu city polity was founded at the end of the 10th Century.

The south-eastern part of Dahomey where Ketu is sited was apparently inhabited by the so-called Ewe-stock (i.e. the Adja, the Fon and Ewe) before the arrival of King Ede, the founder of the Ketu polity, in the area. Not certain about which peoples were in possession of the land of Ketu before Ede's arrival, Parrinder writes, "The present elders at Ketu think that the aborigines were Fon people, the people of the later Dahomey kingdom, related to the Ewe, who for centuries were neighbours and finally destroyers of Ketu. But the Fon themselves have traditions of migrations in these early times.

"There are traces of ancient dwellings in the region of Ketu. At the village of Idahin, some fifteen miles north-east of Ketu, there are old graves dug into the laterite rock, of a kind that is no longer made today, and that the present Yoruba and Fon inhabitants agree in ascribing to unknown aborigines. Another ruined village, called Ewe, a few miles to the North of Ketu, has graves, mounds, cisterns, ruined fortifications and fragments of pottery. The people of Ketu call this Ile-shin, the house of Shin. They say that it was inhabited when Ketu was founded, but later abandoned during the wars, its inhabitants taking refuge in Ketu. A human sacrifice was made at the foundation of Ketu of one of the inhabitants of Ewe."[8]

On the basis of this passage the following conclusions could be drawn:

1. That the Ewe, the Adja and the Fon were not part of the

---

4 *Op. Cit.*, p. 47, the old name "Dahomey" will be used in the subsequent pages of this contribution.
5 Westermann, D., pp. 233–34.
6 Parrinder. E., 1956, p 24
7 He was still alive in 1956.
8 Parrinder, E., 1956, p. 16.

Ede-led Yoruba group which founded Ketu city in the 10th Century.

2. That the Ewe-stock had arrived possibly several hundred years in the land of Ketu before the Yoruba intrusion but became a minority because of the superior numerical strength of the Yoruba.

3. That the Ewe-stock (the Adja, the Fon and Ewe) were apparently forced to migrate to western Dahomey and Togo because of the Yoruba invasion and bitter wars that characterized it.

4. That the village Ewe,[9] "a few miles to the North of Ketu" referred to by Parrinder, could have been an Ewe settlement,[9] and that the cisterns, ruined fortifications and pottery are an indication of a high cultural development of the Ewe-stock in the land of Ketu before the arrival of the Yoruba.

Our discussions so far have not thrown any clear light on the origin, i.e. the cradle of the Ewe. Bertho sees the Ewe people as coming from Ife with Ketu as the first halt in their journey to the West. He writes, "The unanimous traditions of the principal groups which now populate lower Dahomey and lower Togo: Adja, Allada-nu, Quatchi, Ewe, etc., indicate clearly that their ancestors came from the East, and they allow us to localize four successive stages in their march towards the West: 1. Yoruba country . . . 2. The region of Ketu . . . 3. The fortified town of Tado in Togo . . . 4. The fortified town of Nuatja (Notsie) in Togo."[10] King Agokoli III, the present ruler of Notsie in the Republic of Togo, seems to confirm Bertho's claim; according to the King the real cradle of the Ewe-stock (the Ewe, the Adja and the Fon) was Lofi in the East. From Lofi they migrated to Oyo; they left the latter for Ketu from where they "finally" migrated to Wla in lower Dahomey, Tado and Notsie (Nuatja) in southern Togo.[11]

If it is true that Lofi and Ife are identical as the author and some of his informants suspect, or even if they were names of two different geographical locations in the Yoruba country, could one conclude that the Ewe stock was originally Yoruba? If yes, why do the Yoruba and the Ewe speak different languages today? Or was the Ewe language developed after the migration of the Ewe from Ketu? Or could the Ewe language have been the language of a secret society of Ife origin which played an important role in the religious life of the Ketu Ewe? If yes, was the section of

[9] The author is inclined to suspect that this settlement (called "Ewe") was named after the Ewe ethnic group. In human history towns, villages and capitals have borne the names of their respective countries and vice versa. Brasilia derives from Brazil. Togo is a village in the Republic of Togo. The Republic was named after the village by the German colonial authorities. There are several other examples.

[10] Bertho, J., 1949, pp. 121–123 (quoted by Parrinder, E., 1957, p: 7):

[11] The author had a long interview with the king in December 1976. The author has been unable to trace Lofi on any map; but Ewe historians share his suspicion that Lofi could be Ife. The king was not sure if his ancestors went to Oyo city itself or to some other area of Oyo territory.

4

the Ketu Ewe who migrated westwards dominated by the secret society, a situation which could have diminished the importance of the Yoruba language?

Linguists and historians may examine these possibilities.

The author is, however, inclined to believe (a) that the Ewe-stock (the Ewe, the Adja and the Fon) have never been Yoruba proper and (b) that they were once a minority in Yoruba-domina-ted Western Nigeria.

Migration from Ketu

It is not known when exactly the Ewe exodus from Ketu occurred though Ewe oral tradition clearly describes the important routes of the migration. Boahen, however, suggests that the Ewe might have left Ketu in the 15th century together with the Ga who had joined them from the East.[12] The Ewe, we are told, left Ketu in two major groups due to constant wars and raids in the area. According to Spieth the groups were originally two numerically strong sibs.[13] One sib inhabited two areas in what is now south-eastern Togo, namely Tado along the Mono River and Notsie (Nua-tja) between the Haho and Zio rivers. The other group which had also moved in the western direction finally chose Adele as their new home territory—Dogbonyigbo was their most important settle-ment. The Anlo, Be and the Fon were sub-groups of the Dogbonyi-gbo. The Fon left them after serious conflicts and built a new township called Wla (Allada). Akinjogbin dates the foundation of Allada to 1575.[14] Later the Anlo and Be also left and joined their kin in Notsie.

The Notsie Ewe, the sources indicate,[15] migrated from Notsie at the turn of the 16th century because of the growing intolerable tyranny of King Agokoli I, the then divine absolute ruler of Notsie. Some other sources, however, suggest that the exodus from Notsie occurred in about 1670.[16]

The Political and Social Structure of Notsie

In the absence of detailed concrete data on the socio-political organizations of Tado and Wla, it is not possible to make an ade-quate analysis to that effect. An attempt is, however, made to reconstruct the social political pattern of Notsie because of the availability of useful facts (already known) and new data recently collected by the author on Notsie.

Notsie was a large, walled city[17] with small, scattered settlements (sub-units of the Notsie political structure) outside the city walls. In times of war or raids the population of the satellite settlements sought refuge within the strongly built walls.

12 Boahen, A., 1966, p. 64.
13 Spieth J., p. 47. See also Wiegrabbe, P. (ed.) 1963, p. 18.
14 Akinjogbin, I. 1971, p. 313.
15 Westermann, D., pp. 405–406.
16 Wiegrabe, P. (ed.) 1963, p. 23:

Patrilineally organized kinship groups constituted at the same time the political sub-units which were directly responsible to a central authority embodied in the king of Notsie.[18] The king was the highest political authority in Notsie. He was a divine ruler with absolute powers partly rooted in stringent taboos. For example. the king never went bare-footed. His feet were not supposed to touch the bare ground. According to oral tradition drought or flood occurred if this taboo was violated. In other words, the king, who was never deposed, could cause famine and mass destructions at will. It was forbidden to see the Notsie king. Anybody approaching him, even his closest attendants and executive ministers or counsellors, had to do so with their backs turned to him. During his meals there must be absolute silence in the royal palace. The violation of any of these taboos was punishable by death. Any child who heard him cough would die instantly. All sandals had to be left outside, i.e. at the gate of the palace. The king left the palace only during the night. Anybody who came in his way during any of his nocturnal perambulations was executed without delay.[19]

The king of Notsie was helped in his administration by an executive and an administrative council. The administrative council comprised all clan heads in Notsie, while the executive council, smaller in size, was formed by the most important office holders, mostly selected from the administrative council. While every able-bodied man in Notsie was a warrior, there was a small standing army of highly efficient soldiers who kept law and order and carried out slave raids on neighbouring ethnic groups. According to Agokoli III, the present political leader of Notsie, the standing army was camped near the king's palace. It was fed by the people of Notsie. Since it was a taboo for the royal household to cultivate food plants or keep farms, the army, considered as part of the household, stayed away from all kinds of agricultural activity.

Each kinship unit, at the same time a political sub-unit of the Notsie polity, had a *fiazikpui*, an ancestral holy stool kept by the head of the kinship unit. All holy ancestral stools were subordinate to the king's stool.

---

[17] F. C. Akoli claims (his claim is based on a traveller's report) that the height and width of the Notsie walls were 4.6– m and 7.5–9 m respectively (Akoli, F 1963, p. 24). The author measured the width of the foundation wall cut through at two different points during his visit to Notsie in Dec. 1976: It was 3 metres.

[18] The kinship units in Notsie today are Alinu, Adzigo, Agbaladome, Kli. Tegbe, Adinu, Wuto, Anekpeko (the royal clan) Agokoli III claims that they have been the only kinship-units in Notsie since the establishment of the city.

[19] The data on the divine power of the king were collected by the author in Notsie in Dec. 1976. Notsie still has a divine king, apart from a political one who is Agokoli III. The post of the political king was created during French colonial rule. It is the political king who communicates personally with the government and the people of Notsie. Today, the spiritual king, who is never seen, is still surrounded by the same old taboos.

The Economic Structure of Notsie

No attempt has been made by scholars of Ewe history and culture to depict analytically the sub-structure of Notsie society. It is therefore extremely difficult to assess the level of the forces of production and how they related to the relations of production.

According to the Notsie informants of the author, hunting, agriculture and handicrafts were the main economic branches. Fishing was later introduced into the Notsie area by the Anexo people. *Eli* (millet) was the staple food; rice and yam, the informants say, had been growing wild in Notsie before the arrival of the Ewe in the area. While Westermann denies the Notsie Ewe any knowledge in iron works,[20] Notsie oral tradition indicates that iron-smelting and black-smithing were practised early in Notsie. Future archaeological findings may throw some light on the early technology in the area. We should, however, remember that the Ewe culture was part of the Yoruba culture area where bronze technology had been an old tradition.

Weaving, carving, black-smithing, iron-smelting were the most important trades. The main implements in use were the cutlass, axe, hoe, bow and arrow, and the gun which was introduced during the Slave Trade.

Trade was a fairly developed institution within the walls of Notsie, with women playing a dominant role in the exchange mechanisms. External trade developed in the course of the Slave trade. Though the present political ruler of Notsie denies that his dynasty was ever involved in the Slave Trade, other Ewe informants within and outside Notsie emphasise the more or less monopolistic role the Notsie royal house played in the trade.[21] According to these sources the hazards connected with the trade were serious contradictions which also contributed to the exodus from Notsie during the rule of Agokoli I. Stone money was first used; then cowries *(cyprea moneta Z)*. Internal and external trade was controlled by the King who also received tributes in kind at the harvest of every crop. Certain parts of every wild animal killed had to be sent to the royal household through the clan head of the hunter.

The nuclear family was the production and consumption unit. There were already rudiments of social division of labour.

The Exodus from Notsie

Causes

Ewe oral tradition[22] says that there was a high rate of criminality in the Notsie community. People disappeared mysteriously. Agokoli

---

[20] Westermann, D., p. 234.
[21] We should remember that Notsie was in the heart of the so-called Slave Coast. According to the latest data collected by research workers of the University of Cape Coast, populations outside the Notsie polity attracted the greed of the Notsie kings who subjected them to regular raids and plunder. Captives taken were made slaves and sold to European slavers.
[22] This information was given to the author by King Agokoli III, present political ruler of Notsie.

7

I, the then divine ruler of Notsie, attributed the disappearances to clandestine raids by slavers from outside. He accordingly directed that the whole city be walled. After this difficult task was completed people were still disappearing. King Agokoli became suspicious that old people in the city were either involved in the slave trade secretly or were killing people for ritual purposes. He therefore ordered the execution of all old people in the city. An old lady[23] who had escaped the massacre was kept in a secret place by the people. When the executioners returned to report to the king on their successful mission they were asked to go back and ask the people to perform an impossible task, namely, to prepare a rope out of mud for roofing. The people consulted the old lady who advised them to ask King Agokoli to send them a specimen of a rope made out of mud since they had never seen one. Delighted by the shrewd message Agokoli said to the executioners, "This sagacious request by the people could only emerge from an old, experienced mind". Thus outwitted and not sure what Agokoli would do next, the people of Notsie began to leave the city in large numbers. Before Agokoli knew what was happening the majority had already left. His attempts to hold them back failed.

The mud-rope episode only occasioned the exodus. It is said that the people were generally dissatisfied with the rule of King Agokoli I, and had been planning secretly the mass migration for a fairly long time. For example, women had been assigned the task by leaders of the exodus plot to be soaking daily selected points in the massive city walls with waste water. It was at these wetted points that openings were then made and used as emergency exits by the escapees.

The Migration Routes

To be able to successfully resist any eventual attempt by King Agokoli to bring them back to Notsie the escaping Ewe covered the first phase of their journey together. They split up into three main units only when any possible attack by Agokoli's standing warriors was considered very remote. One unit went to the South,[24] another to the North while the third group drifted in the middle direction, i.e. to the area between South and West. Further sub-divisions of these units and their final settlement ended the adventurous journey.

[23] Another version of the story indicates that it was an old man called Teglee (see Wiegrabe, P. (ed.), 1963, p. 21).
[24] The sub-units of the southern group were Be, Togo, Abobo, Weta, Anlo (including Taviefe), Kliko, Some, Ave, Fenyi, Afife, Mañ, Tseme, Agave, Tanyigbe, Tokokoe—The units of the middle group were Ho. Akoviefe, Takla, Kpenoe, Hodzo, Klefe, Sokode, Abutia, Adaklu and Akomu. The first four sub-groups were closely related and had constituted a single sub-clan in Notsie. They therefore maintained a strong solidarity throughout the long, hazardous journey. The north group consisted of Gbi, Kpele, Awudome, Ge, Atsyem, Alavanyo, Kpando, We, Leklebi, Logba, Saviefe, Dzolo, Akome, Kpedze, Matse, Kpetsi, Wodze, etc. (See Wiegrabe, P. (ed.), p. 25 ff).

The splitting up of the Notsie Ewe during the journey on kinship basis partly led to the development of about 130 small autonomous political units. In spite of the spatial separation there has been (ever since) the consciousness of oneness among the Ewe generally and particularly between sets of *duwo*,[25] i.e. autonomous political units which formerly constituted one and the same sub-unit in the centrally ruled Notsie political set-up.

[25] For example the special brotherly and friendly relationship today between the Peki Ewe and their kin at Hohoe and other places; between the Anlo and their kin at Taviefe and Tsevie, etc.

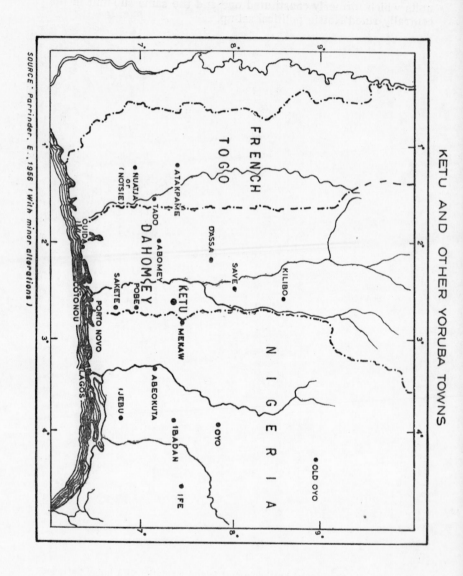

KETU AND OTHER YORUBA TOWNS

SOURCE : Parrinder, E., 1956 (with minor alterations)

PART II

THE ECONOMY OF THE POST-NOTSIE EWE SOCIETY

Agriculture

Peasant Agriculture based on shifting cultivation constituted the basis of existence in the Central Plains and the hilly areas while agricultural activities in the form of intensive cultivation and garden farming were genera'ly practised on the coastal banks.

In January and February the Ewe cleared the bush or forest, lopping the branches of small trees which were then burnt up a few days later. In grassy areas the bush was usually burnt in the dry season; the clearing was thus facilitated. The ashes were left on the new fields to serve as fertilizers.

Two sowing seasons were observed:
The first season was from February to the end of May. Crops cultivated were yams *(dioscorea alata)*, maize *(zea mays)*, beans *(phaselus vulgaries)*, okro *(hibiscus esculentus)*, groundnuts *(arachis hypogaea)*, onion *(allium cepa)*, gourds *(laganaria vulgaris)* and other vegetables, taro *(colocasia antiquorum)*, Manioc *(manihot utilissinia)*, cola *(cola acuminata)*, coconut *(cocos nuicifera)*, banana and plantain *(musa sapientum, musa paradisiaca)*, oil palm *(elaeis guineesis)*, and several other fruits. The second sowing season began in July and ended in September; all the above-named crops, with the exception of yams and taro, were planted again.

Maize was harvested at the end of June and September, and yam between July and October. The vegetables were usually reaped and gathered three to four months after the time of sowing. Plantain and banana could only be ready for harvest after one and a half years.

In some areas in the southern part of the Central Plains where geographical conditions did not favour the growth of yams, taro and other root crops, maize and manioc were cultivated. Beans and peanuts were other main crops grown in the area. The area in question, i.e. the southern skirt of the Central Plains, was one of the most productive areas in Ewe-land. The following export data collected by Herold throw some light on surplus production in the area.

1890	...	...	...	...	638 000 kg
1891	...	...	...	...	276 000 kg
1892	...	...	...	...	2 000 kg

maize, peanuts and copra were exported.[1] The 1890 figures show that surplus production in the area could be fairly high at the

11

beginning of the German colonial rule in Togo. The following constitute the reasons for the apparently high production:
1. There was enough land; 2. the amount of rainfall in the area (700 mm yearly) was particularly favourable for peanut cultivation; 3. already in the pre-colonial time there was market in the area for foodstuffs, a situation which served as an incentive for food production. Rice, already cultivated by the Ewe in Notsie, was further grown after the exodus.

Most important rice-growing areas were Logba and Avatime. According to Herold pre-colonial rice production was so high that a lot of rice was sent from the interior to the Coast where it was sold cheaper than imported rice.[2]

Yam was an important staple, especially in the interior of the country. Yam cultivation involved 8–9 months hard labour. Under normal environmental conditions many an Ewe farmer could be sure of good yield on which he could depend till the next harvest season. Fies writes, "Anybody in Ho, for example, who could not bring home 800–1,000 yams a year was regarded as a shirker. A successful farmer and his dependants did not only depend on the yam fufu all the year round, but a lot of the harvested yams were also sold so that several other requirements of the family could be met."[3]

About 45 lb of yams cost 50 farthings (about 26 pesewas) in 1883; in 1903 the price increased by 150%.

Though manioc (cassava) is widely cultivated today throughout Ewe-land, it was more or less disregarded by the Ewe till the twenties of this century.

Onion cultivation was practised, especially on the Anlo Peninsula where the crop was raised on the basis of intensive cultivation. The Anlo Peninsula and Anexo are regarded by the Ewe as the cradles of their highly respected onion culture.[4]

Sand and clay sediments which settled in the lagoons in the Volta Delta characterized the soil in the Keta lagoons. The natural conditions favourable for the growth of onion were thus non-existent in the area. The onion farmer, however, broke up the stiff, tenacious earth during the dry season, and mixed the soil with sand there-by diluting its salty components. Beds, separated from one another by paths and drainage-gutters, were then made. The farmer forked the beds and mixed the forked earth with broken shells. Animal dung brought in from the Central Plains and small species of fish and fish powder were then added as manure. Small water holes dug at regular distances on each bed served as water reservoirs. The farmer depended on the water holes for quite a long time.[5]

---

[1] Herold, B., 1893, p. 268.
[2] Op. cit.
[3] Fies, K., 1903, p. 268. (My own translation)
[4] Manshard, W., 1961, p. 46.
[5] The Keta onion farmers still use the same old intensive method of onion cultivation. (See Manshard, W., 1961, p. 46.)

12

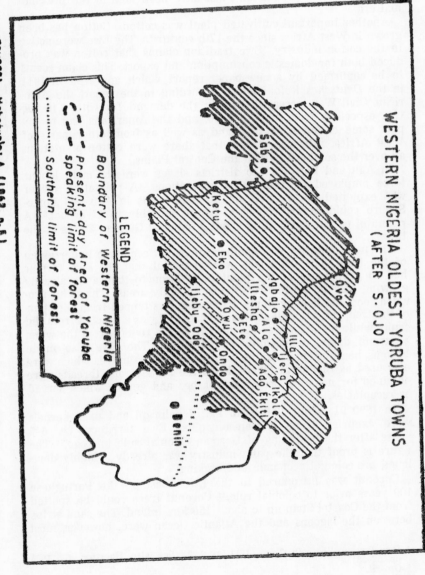

WESTERN NIGERIA OLDEST YORUBA TOWNS
(AFTER S. OJO)

LEGEND

—— Boundary of Western Nigeria

- - - Present-day Area of Yoruba
speaking limit of forest

- - - Southern limit of forest

.... Southern limit of forest

Sabe

Ketu

Eko

Oyo

Ila

Agbajo
Ijera
Illesha
Ala
Ikole
Ete
Owu
Ado Ekiti
Ijebu-Ode
Ondo

Benin

13

Labour productivity in the onion economy might have been quite high. According to Manshard 3,500 kg of onions per acre is a normal yield today. And since the method of cultivation has scarcely changed production must have been high in the pre-colonial era.

Another important cultivated plant was cotton. Cotton has been grown in West Africa since the 17th century.[6] The Ewe were active in the cotton industry. Ewe tradition claims that cotton was produced both for domestic consumption and export. This claim seems to be confirmed by a newspaper report which appeared in 1911 in the *Deutsches Kolonialblatt.* According to the report the American Civil War increased sharply the demand for cotton in the U.S. especially from 1865 to 1870, and the Americans had to import some cotton from Ewe-land as well as from other parts of West Africa. The report says that there were cotton plantations all over the southern part of the Central Plains.

In Agu and Porto-Seguro districts slaves were the main labour force employed on the cotton plantations.[7] A plantation owner who exploited 40–45 slaves on his plantations in Agu and Porto-Seguro could export 200 kg of cotton monthly to Liverpool.[8] A pound of cotton was costing about 2 imperial German Marks at the time[9].

The palm industry was another important economic undertaking of the Ewe. The palm tree was so useful that the Ewe farmer had to grow more of the plant in addition to thousands already growing wild in the Central Plains and hilly areas. The palm provided food and healing items. Palm wine was tapped from the stem of the tree; red palm oil and palm kernel oil was extracted from the fruits while medicine was obtained from the roots. From the wine, a strong drink, *akpeteshie,* was distilled. The Ewe also made brooms, baskets, etc. from the branches of the palm tree which were also used as roofing material. From the roots strong threads were obtained for mending broken calabashes and gourds which served as receptacles.

In 1890/91, about 13,936,315 kg. of palm oil and palm kernels were exported from German-controlled Ewe territory, i.e. 6–7 years after the beginning of German colonial rule in Togo.[10] The figure is proof that the palm industry was already a highly developed pre-colonial economic undertaking.

Coconut was introduced to the Ewe Coast by the Portuguese 100 years prior to colonial rule.[11] Coconut trees could be spotted from the Coastal Strip up to about 150 km. inland. The sand strips between the lagoons and the Atlantic Ocean were, however, most

---

[6] *Der Baumwollbau in Togo,* 1911, p. 229 (See also Haertter, G., 1906 pp. 52–53).
[7] *Op. cit.*
[8] *Op. cit.*
[9] *Op. cit.*
[10] Goldberg, 1892, p. 170
[11] *Op. cit.*

favourable for coconut cultivation; in fact the largest plantations are still sited in these areas today.

Goldberg claims that there were about 120,000 coconut trees on the coastal strip in 1892 while the rest of Ewe-land could only account for 10,000 trees in the same year.[12] The data show that the concentration of the copra industry on the coast is not a new development but rather a pre-colonial phenomenon.

The inland Ewe have never taken the copra industry seriously; they have preferred to eat coconut raw. If in 1892 the number of coconut trees in the German-occupied Ewe territory alone, i.e. without the coconut plantations in the English-controlled Ewe areas, was 130,000, then we could imagine the extent to which the coconut industry had developed before colonial rule.

As indicated in the following table most of the coconut plantations were privately owned.[13]

Place of Plantation	Owner	No. of Trees
Lome	Several Individual owners	28 500
	Olympio	13 000
Lome	Individual owners	1 000
Bagida	d'Modeoiros	6 5000
Bagida	Dloff	50 000
Porto Seguro	Individual Private owners	500
—	Individual Private owners	4 2000
Klein Popo Districts	TOTAL	107 700

Cola and rubber were also produced for both internal consumption and export.

Fishing

Fishing was a lucrative economic activity on the Ewe coast and at the southern periphery of the Coastal Plains. High sea and lagoon fishing was already specialized before colonial rule. The Ewe caught fish also in both small and big rivers. Up to the beginning of the 19th century, i.e., several decades after the exodus from Notsie, fishing was only a supplementary economic undertaking. Haertter claims the Coastal Ewe combined fish industry with agriculture and handicrafts.[14] Specialization set in as the coastal fishermen developed and acquired better means of production such as nets, boats and canoes. Earlier, spears, bows and arrows and harpoons had mainly been used.

12 *Op. cit.*
13 *Op. cit.*, p. 169.
14 Haertter, G., 1906, p. 53

15

The pre-colonial Ewe fishermen were conversant with the most important environmental phenomena which in one way or another were relevant to the organisation of fishing. For example, they understood the cyclic movements of different fish species. Haertter writes, "The fisherman knows that when the pleiades *(atifiemi)* appears in the heavens the rainy season begins, and when *avule*, also a constellation, is seen then it is an indication that the rainy season will end in three or four weeks. He knows exactly when the season begins again; in fact, the fisherman even knows in which month a particular fish goes ashore to lay eggs. He is also aware that when a fish called *kafia* leaves the beach for the high seas the rainy season normally comes to an end".[15]

Little is known about the structure of the fishing production units. We could, however, safely assume that, at the early stage of the fishing economy, i.e. the time when the spear, bow and arrow were mainly used and the fish industry was a mere supplement to agriculture only men were engaged in fishing. Female labour was apparently drawn into it when, through the introduction of better and more sophisticated technology, labour productivity was raised and the industry became specialised.

Women dried and conserved the fish. From January to June when their husbands were busy fishing up-stream women undertook oyster-dredging along the southern banks of River Volta.

Non-consanguineal fishing production units apparently emerged only when specialisation in the trade reached an appreciable level of development. According to Manoukian, fishing companies were the production units.[16] A fishing company which comprised several fulltime fishermen had one or two boats. Lagoon and river fishing was more or less a one-man undertaking for the most important instrument of labour, the so-called *asabu* net, used here, was handled by a single person.

Data on the level of labour productivity in the fishing industry are scanty. It is accordingly almost impossible to indicate the amount of fish caught with a specific instrument at a particular place within a time unit. The following quotation shows that a fairly high level of labour productivity was reached already in the pre-colonial period. "It would have been a pity if hundreds and thousands of surplus fish often caught a day had got spoilt. The Ewe fisherman saw in the rays of the sun a good helper; they dried the fish for him within a short time so well that they could be kept days and weeks. By this means he was able to conserve fish for the consumption of his household and for sale in the market. It is in this conserved condition that the fish travelled days inland."[17] Smoking was another form of fish conservation.

---

[15] *Op. cit.* p. 55 (My own translation).
[16] Manoukian, M., 1952, p. 16. Her claim was confirmed by informants in Anlo, who pointed out that the fishing company had been a pre-colonial institution.
[17] Haertter, G., 1906, pp. 51–52. (My own translation).

16

Fishing Rights

The coastal waters, the lagoons, the rivers and rills were communally owned. Fishing communities, families and individuals, however, laid claim temporarily to fishing grounds. This claim was only recognized if nets and creels had been already laid. The so-called *Abla* System allowed private possession of rich fishing grounds in the lagoons. A fence was usually erected in a chosen area in the lagoon; every fence had a number of openings called *xadowo* (about 50–100 per fence). A creel was then positioned at the mouth of every *xado* (*xado* = singular; *xadowo* = plural) to collect escaping fish. Only the owner and his relatives were allowed near the fence. The fishing ground could be inherited. If the owner had several heirs the *xadowo* were usually divided among the heirs. The fishing ground must, however, remain family property.[18]

Nets, creels, boats, canoes, harpoons and other implements could be privately owned. It was easier for the ordinary man to acquire rill, river and lagoon fishing equipment than high sea-fishing implements which could only be acquired by rich people.

While the individual rill, river and lagoon fishermen owned all that they caught, catches made on the sea were usually divided as follows: Net owner—50%; boat owner—25%; fishermen (who provided only labour)—25%.[19]

Fishing inland was an insignificant secondary economic activity. Fish were caught by individuals in rivers.

Hunting

Hunting played an important role in the Ewe economy up to the beginning of the 20th century.[20] The importance of hunting in the earlier time is reflected in several hunting rituals still practised today. The main hunting season was the dry season, i.e. from December to March when the grass was low or burnt.

Forms of hunting were battue, night hunting, trapping. The spatial and periodic distribution of fauna was determined by geographic and seasonal conditions. The elephant, now extinct in South-eastern Ghana and southern Togo, was found usually in the highlands, thick forests, in the savannah, as well as near river banks. The short-legged buffalo and bush pigs preferred mountainous forests and swampy areas. Different species of antelope and monkey, leopard, hyena, crocodile, etc. were abundant. A variety of birds in all colours, from the humming bird to the vulture, was a normal sight throughout Ewe-land. Bow and arrow, different types of trap and gun were the hunting weapons. There

[18] All the information on the Abla-System was given to the author by Anlo-Ewe informants.

[19] *Op. cit.*

[20] The author has seen hundreds of chained jaw bones of wild game killed by hunters of different generations and kept as family souvenirs. The maternal grandfather of the author, one Mr. Dzewu from Tsibu in the Volta Region of Ghana, is alleged to have killed at least 3,000 wild animals—most of them killed at the end of the 19th century.

was no private or family hunting ground within the territory of an autonomous political unit which was called *Du*. All hunting grounds were commonly owned. Hunting in an alien territory was prohibited and in fact was regarded as a serious provocation.

All game killed during a hunting expedition were distributed among the participants; if a hunter (in a one-man expedition) shot or trapped an animal, he shared the meat with the most important hunters in the community, clan heads and with relatives.

Animal Husbandry

With the exception of large cattle herds kept in areas on the coast only small livestock was reared by the Ewe. Goldberg suggests that there were about 640 cattle (mostly in the coastal areas) about 20,000 sheep, 30,000 goats and almost 100,000 pigs in southern Togo in 1892.[21]

Animal husbandry was commercially undertaken only on the Coast. In the interior it was an important supplement to agriculture. Herold writes, "Only in the coastal areas and along important caravan routes do people attempt to rear livestock for commercial purposes. The demand is constantly greater than the supply. Cargo and warships therefore prefer visiting English Keta and Yolukovhe when it comes to buying foodstuffs."[22]

There was no division of labour by sex in the livestock economy.

Salt Industry

The salt industry was a very important economic activity in the lagoon areas. In the dry season men dug wide shallow pits in which the salty water got precipitated after the retreat of the water. The salt deposit was then extracted by women. It was the lagoon areas which supplied the hinterland with salt. The salt grounds were no private property. During the salt season the principle of "first come first served" obtained, that is, in terms of temporary claims to grounds. Individuals who were quick to grab plots in the lagoons at the beginning of the season enjoyed the exclusive right of use throughout the period of salt exploitation.

Handicrafts

Spinning, weaving, iron work, pottery, carving, mat-plaiting, leather work, masonry, were the main handicrafts.[23] There was some degree of semi-regional Specialization in handicrafts, a phenomenon apparently determined by geographical and historical factors. While spinning and weaving were the main handicrafts widely undertaken in the coastal areas, carving, iron work and mat-plaiting were the main inland handicrafts. The people of Akpafu and San-

---

[21] Goldberg. 1892. p. 175.
[22] Herold, B., 1893, p 268. (My own translation).
[23] See Seidel, J., 1895, p. 315; Spieth, J., 1906 pp. 50–51; Herold, B., 1893, pp. 270–271.

trokofi were known for their excellent iron technology. Pottery, widely practised wherever there was enough good quality clay, was a lucrative source of income, especially for the people of Bolu on the coast and of Kpando and Teve in the interior. Kponadzi and Veme in Tongu were also famous for their pottery in Ewe-land. Atakpame was known for its leather-work.[24] Spieth claims that families in a village specialized in different trades "as the history of Matse shows". According to him each village ward in Matse had a specific occupation. There were, for example, hunters' ward, blacksmiths' ward, farmers' ward, etc.[25]

The quality of the pre-colonial Ewe handicrafts was fairly high. The Ewe depended largely on their own handicrafts till the era of colonial rule.

Canstatt, a former German colonial director, assessed the pre-colonial Ewe handicrafts as follows: ". . . the thousand items daily used or those produced by the Ewe for the market, namely handicraft products, awaken our great interest making the level of cultural development of that tribal group on the Slave Coast favourably comparable with that of Western civilization."[26]

While women dominated pottery and spinning, other handicrafts mentioned above were exclusively men's jobs.

Traffic and Trade

Only footpaths and water routes linked villages, districts and regions with one another. The rivers Volta, Mono and Danyi were the most important water routes. The Volta connected on one hand a vast area of the coastal strip with the Ga-Adangbe and on the other these two areas with the western highlands in the Ewe hinterland. Danyi and Mono connected several settlements *(Duwo)* in the eastern and western parts of the Central Plains.

Different canoe types were the only vessels used. Animals as means of transport, such as the horse, the camel and the donkey, were not used by the Ewe. Long distances were covered on foot. According to Mote, a journey from Kebu, a former rubber-trading centre in the Central Plains, to Keta lasted 8 days. The distance was 128 kilometers.[27]

Ewe trade underwent a rapid development in the post-migration period because of favourable geographic and historical conditions in their new home environments. The more diverse nature of the new home-land made the diversification of production possible; more internally produced items could be consequently introduced into trade. For example, the coastal Ewe traded in fish and salt with peasant communities, while the inland Nkonya regularly supplied canoes to the fish industry on the Coast and along the Volta. The Nkonya canoe-makers fell big trees, usually the satin, a few

[24] Herold, B., 1893, p. 273.
[25] Spieth, J., 1906, pp. 50–52.
[26] Canstatt, D., 1900, p. 551. See also Seidel, H., 1900, p. 148; Herold, L., 1893, p. 277.
[27] Mote, S., 1963, p. 63.

3

kilometers from the banks of the Volta upland where they made the canoes. Herold points out that the Nkonya dominated the canoe trade on the Ewe Coast and along the Volta.[28] Trade in iron goods, the production of which was dominated by Akpafu, was wide-spread.

There were big markets in important settlements which linked up commercially districts and regions. Some of these markets were located at Dzofe, Nyagbo, Anfoega and Dukrudza along the Volta and Danyi.[29] Dukrudza was an important commercial base for Ada traders on their way to Krachi. Other market centres were Kpando, Adaklu, Tove, Ho, Kpedze, Dzelukofe, Tado, Kpalime and a number of coastal towns, such as Porto Seguro, Anecho, Lome, Keta, etc.[30]

Trade entered a new phase of development as a result of Ewe European contacts—the pre-colonial era ended in 1874 and 1884 when Britain and Germany formally proclaimed their colonial rule respectively over the Ewe. During this early contact period trade expanded; coastal traders for the first time introduced European goods into their trade system selling them in addition to the traditional commodities like salt and fish, etc. to peasant communities in all parts of Ewe-land. Goods produced by the peasants were taken to the coast by the same traders. This means that a class of full-time traders was already in existence in the pre-colonial period.

Pearls, small mirrors, tobacco, matches, guns, gun-powder, gin, weinbrand were the main commodities Europeans brought to the so-called Slave Coast. Ewe chiefs profited a lot from the slave trade between the 16th and the beginning of the 19th centuries.[31]

Cowries were the medium of exchange. Coastal Ewe traders exchanged at times salt, tobacco, gun-powder and guns directly for slaves in the interior, and they were then sold to Europeans. Haertter claims that in the last days of the slave trade these coastal traders made a profit of about 100 German marks on every slave child.[32]

Every 4th or 5th days was a market day in some trading centres (mentioned above) and numerous Ewe villages.

Superstructure of the Post-Notsie Society

In spite of the complex nature of the economy in the new Ewe home-land super-structural traits such as kinship structure and religion remained intact. The higher level of the productive forces now attained, led, however, to the emergence of new social contradictions.

---

[28] Herold, B., 1893, pp. 274–275.
[29] Mote, S., 1968, p. 60.
[30] Op. cit.
[31] King Ladzekpo of Anexo, a notorious slaver, went to Liverpool 1860 by a slave ship to sell his own slaves (Haertter, G., 1901/2, p. 494).
[32] Haertter, G., 1901/2, p. 442.

Kinship Structure

Hlɔ (Sib)[1]

The *Hlɔ*, which consisted of several *kowo*, was the largest unit in the Ewe kinship system. It was, however, found only among the Anlo and Glidzi Ewe on the coast. The members of a *hlɔ* did not constitute an organic unit in spatial and economic terms. They inhabited different areas and established the common *hlɔ* identity by tracing their descent from a common patrilineal ancestor, though it was not always easy to clearly define the consanguineal relations and genealogical positions of individual members of the *hlɔ*. Each *hlɔ* was represented in the Anlo and Glidzi capitals by its head.

One or more taboos and vendetta obligations were some of the centripetal factors which strengthened the unity and moral solida‑ rity of the *hlɔ*. Women married into the *hlɔ* were not regarded or accepted as *hlɔ* members. Social, and to a limited degree, eco‑ nomic solidarity, constituted functionally the most vital ideal of each *hlɔ*. The *hlɔ*-head was a link between the members of his *hlɔ* and the king. Royal instructions and directives were passed through the *hlɔ*-heads to the subjects. Organization of ceremonies and festivals, hearing of cases involving kinship units within a *hlɔ* were some of the most important functions of the head of each *hlɔ*.

Kɔ or To (Maximal Lineage)[2]

The *Kɔ* was the largest kinship unit among other Ewe groups.[3] Descent was traced patrilineally. The agnatic nucleus of each *kɔ* lived in a specific, well-defined territory. Though she could partake in the religious ceremonies of the *kɔ* of her husband, a woman married from outside the *kɔ*, though socially fully integrated, was never accepted as a true *kɔ* member. The woman's body had to be collected by her own *kɔ* when she passed away, so that her soul could go to her own ancestors. Endogamous unions were allowed, provided the consanguineal relationship of the partners concerned was not so close as to break laid-down incestuous taboos. Every *kɔ* bore a specific name, had a common territory and specified land, as well as several gods.

The most important functions of the *Kɔ* head were:
1. To organize and supervise festivals, rituals and funerals of the *kɔ* members.
2. To see to it that functional sanctions and ideals such as social and material solidarity, socialization responsibilities, etc. were strictly adhered to by all members.

---

[1] Mudock's kinship terminology is adopted here.
Nukunya uses the term "clan" instead of "sib".
(Nukunya, G., 1969, p. 21).
See also Asamoa, A., 1971, pp. 173–176.
[2] I shall use *Kɔ* throughout. *Kɔwo* is the plural form of *Kɔ*.
[3] See "Political Structure" below.

3. To settle disputes between individual *Kɔ* members on one hand and between sub-units of the *kɔ* on the other.
4. To represent and defend the *Kɔ* and its members in and against all political and other kinship units within a *Du*. In other words, the *kɔ* head acted as the channel of contact between his *kɔ* and other kinship units and political organs within a *Du*. Backed by his *kɔ* the *kɔ*-head served as the defence counsel of any accused *kɔ* member at the chief's or king's court.
5. To mediate between the dead and living members of the *Kɔ*.
6. To allocate land to members for farming and housing.

Sporadic gifts, such as farm products and parts of hunted game, voluntary work by *Kɔ members on the farms of the Kɔ*-head, were the economic privileges enjoyed by the latter. Though they could be regarded as part of the surplus product of the *kɔ* these material privileges were insignificant in terms of quantity and wealth accumulation.

Avedufe (Major Lineage)[4]

This kinship unit was a sub-unit within the patrilineally structured *kɔ*. A section of the male members of an *Avedufe* constituted a localized residential nucleus of the unit thereby serving as the pivot around which the whole *Avedufe* turned. Other male members of the *Avedufe* could live in any part of the territory of the *Kɔ* of which the *Avedufe* was a sub-unit. All members of an *avedufe* could easily trace their consanguineal relationships and their common genealogical heritage. Both endogamous and exogamous marriages were permitted; women married from outside the *Avedufe* were not accepted as members.

The functions and privileges of the *Avedufe* head were similar to those of the *kɔ* head.

Fome (Minimal Lineage)

The *Fome* was a patrilineally structured, extended family, consisting of two or more nuclear families.

Usually bearing the same surname, the members of the patrilineally organized Ewe extended family could precisely trace their consanguineal relationship to one another without difficulty. The patriarch of the extended family was either a grandfather or a great-grandfather whose male descendants formed the nucleus of the *Fome*. The oldest male member, in agnatic terms, succeeded the patriarch after the latter's death.

The *Fome* members, excluding women married into the unit from outside, were either brothers and sisters or cousins of different grades. First grade parallel and cross-cousin marriages were prohibited; consanguineal marriages beyond the first-cousins grade were however allowed, if not encouraged. Thus women endo-

---

[4] The coastal Ewe call it *Afedo*. (See Nukunya, G., p. 26).

gamously married in an *avedufe* which comprised several extended families *(Fomewo)* belonged to the same minimal lineage as their husbands.

Though extended families, especially small ones, lived in a common compound, generally speaking most nuclear families lived outside the residential domain of the patriarch. With few exceptions the *Fome* was not a production and consumption unit in spite of the well-defined economic and social solidarity that characterized the unit. The head of each *Fome* was obliged, among other things, to settle disputes between his kin members, organise rituals and represent his extended family in the larger kinship units.

The nuclear family

The nuclear family was the smallest kinship unit in pre-colonial Ewe society. Spieth claims that monogamy was originally the only form of marriage practised by the Ewe.[5] He maintains that polygyny developed in course of time because of the following factors:

1. Uneasiness of husbands about bodily, intellectual and spiritual defects of their first wives.
2. Superstitious ideas about menstruation.[6]
3. The desire to have many children.
4. Inability of the first wife to do farm work.
5. Barrenness of the first wife.
6. The wish of many women to regularly visit their parents and stay with them for some time especially when they were expecting a baby.

7. Sexual dissatisfaction.[7]

The nuclear family constituted usually the production and consumption unit, though among the fishing population on the coast a larger kin group could form a production but not necessarily consumption unit at the same time. According to Von Werder even within a nuclear family functioning as a production and consumption unit only part of the fruits of the labour of the grown-up individuals was contributed to the maintenance of the family as a whole; the remaining part was kept as personal property.[8]

Fies seems to be of the same opinion when he writes: "The father cultivates usually a small row of 20 to 30 yams for his young son. The heaviest labour required is provided by the father, the son must however keep the row always tidy by regularly getting rid of weeds. The boy can sell the yields as his personal property

---

5 Spieth, J., 1906. pp 57–58.
6 Women were regarded as polluted during menstruation. Due to the alleged inhygienic nature of the menstrual process, women undergoing menstruation had to l've in huts especially erected for them at the outskirts of the settlement and must not come in contact with priests, men and chiefs.
7 It was an offence to co-habit with a woman during the entire period of her pregnancy. Sexual intercourse with the woman was discouraged till the new-born baby was weaned.
8 Werder, p. Von. (year of publication not indicated), p. 67.

if he so wishes. He can either buy clothes with or invest the money in poultry . . . The wife also gets two or three rows, about 60 – 80 yams as her personal property and can dispose of the yields as she wishes."[9]

The economic independence of the nuclear family, though an indication of a high level of the productive forces at the time, did not negate the economic and moral solidarity within the extended family and other larger kinship units of which the extended family formed an integral part. Members of different nuclear families helped one another mutually on the farm.

Social Stratification

Westermann identifies four main social strata in pre-colonial Ewe-society, namely (a) the nobility, i.e. chiefs and their elders, (b) the free citizens, (c) bondsmen and (d) slaves.

As mentioned above private acquisition of means of production, such as cattle, boats, nets, etc. was in the bud and it was mainly chiefs and professional traders who acquired this kind of private property. The acquisition of important means of production as private property by chiefs strengthened the already high social position of the nobility which hinged primarily on birth. The free subject enjoyed the right of usufruct in terms of lineage land as the most important means of production. He could by means of his surplus production in land cultivation, acquire means of production, such as cattle, boats and trade capital. In other words, the free citizen or subject could be rich or poor materially. As a matter of fact the nobility budded off from the stratum of free subjects. It is, however outside the domain of this paper to trace historically the development of the nobility.

The bondsmen were either aliens who enjoyed the right of land use for which they had to give the local chief yearly tributes in kind or indigenous inhabitants who placed themselves under the protection of a local chief against vendetta or because of indebtedness.[10] A free citizen unable to pay his debts in cash could pay his creditor in labour; such a person was also regarded as a bondsman.

The first generation of alien bondsmen and their immediate posterity were regarded as aliens. Only after several generations were the descendants granted native status.

Slaves were mainly acquired by means of purchase; others were war captives. Slaves were usually aliens; scarcely were indigenes enslaved. A certain percentage of those sold into slavery were anti-social elements, such as incorrigible thieves, and others who had lost the protection of their kinship units because of crime. Intentional killing of a slave was regarded as murder and was accordingly punished. The progeny of slaves bore slave status and could be sold.

9 Fies, K., 1903, p. 267. (My own translation)
10 See Westermann, D., 1935, p. 125.

Matrimonial unions between slaves and free subjects were possible, though the children of such a wedlock were still slaves even if their mother was a free subject. If vice versa, i.e. if the father was a free citizen then the children enjoyed automatically free citizen status because of the patrilineal system of descent practised by the Ewe.

Westermann points out that slaves had to work 4 days a week for their owners and that traders who owned slaves usually gave the latter "capital" thus enabling them to eventually free themselves by paying a sum of money equal to the price of two slaves.[11] Slaves laboured usually on plantations, and in the fishing industry; handicrafts, palm-wine-tapping, cattle-rearing, etc. were other areas of slave activity. Oral traditions indicate that in most parts of Ewe-land slaves were no more required by their owners to provide labour when they (slaves) got married.

Political Structure

The *Du* was the largest Ewe political unit.[12] The members of a *Du* inhabited a clearly defined territory and had traditions of a common origin dating back to Notsie, if not to Ketu. Before colonial rule the Ewe had about 130 *Duwo*.[13] Several villages called *Dutawo* or *Gbɔtawo*[14] in Ewe constituted a *Du*. One of these villages was the *Fiadu*, i.e. the capital where the paramount chief or king was resident.

The administration of a *Du* was the direct responsibility of an executive council called *Fiahawo*. The council consisted of the *Dufiagã*, i.e. the paramount chief, the sub-chiefs who ruled the *Gbɔtawo* and their most important officers, such as the *Tsyiame* (spokesman) and *Asafohene*.[15]

The *Sɔhewo* (the Commoners' Council) represented and safeguarded the interests of all subjects below the rank of *Fiahawo*. The *Sɔhewo* constituted the most effective opposition group to the *Fiahawo*.

The highest administrative organ was the *Dumegãwo*, comprising the *Fiahawo*, several lineage elders from all the *Gbɔtawo* and

11 Westermann, D., 1935, p. 126.
12 *Du* is equivalent to *Oman* in Ashanti. There were larger political units than the *Duwo*; their importance is, now and then, over-emphasized in the literature. These political organizations, usually comprising several *duwo* and with features of a central authority, were only provisionally formed, normally during wars. For example during the Akwamu-Ewe wars (1828–1833) 30 independent *duwo* formed an alliance under king Kodze Dey, ruler of Peki. During the Ewe-Ashanti wars, (1869) Agotime, Atikpoe, Adame, Nyive, Yokele, Kpele, Tokokoe, Lume, Sokode, Abutia and Awudome, all independent *duwo*, became allies under the supreme command of Kete Kofi, king of Ho. These alliances were dissolved after the wars. There were, however, a few permanent political organizations with a central authority reminiscent of that of Notsie. Anlo, Keve, Glidzi and Agu fell into this category.

15 *Duwo* is the plural form of *Du*.
14 Plural of *Gbɔta*. Plural nouns are formed in Ewe by adding *wo*.
15 See pp. 26–29.

the *Sɔhewo*. The Council of *Dumegãwo* was convened only for very serious deliberations in terms of, e.g. war, important festivals, crimes, such as murder and treason.

Every *Gbɔta* within the *Du* had its own chief, its own executive council and *Dumegãwo* of which the *Gbɔta* branch of the *Sɔhewo* formed part. All these *Gbɔta* power organs functioned mainly on the *Gbɔta* level. Their functions were, however, closely watched and controlled by the executive council of *Dumegãwo* on the *Du* level.

The *Fiadu*, i.e. the seat of the paramount chief, was not necessarily the largest or economically the most important *Gbɔta*. Only historical and political considerations reflecting the traditions of the paramountcy were decisive in its choice as the seat of administration.

Important Officers

Dufiagã (Paramount Chief)

The office of the *Dufiagã* was hereditary within a specific kinship unit, though there were cases where two or more kinship units alternately filled the post.[16] The hereditary nature of the post of the *Dufiagã*, of those of his sub-chiefs and almost all other officers within the Ewe traditional political hierarchy was an expression of the existence of a fairly developed nobility. The members of the royal lineage were either descendants of sub-chiefs in Notsie or of outstanding heroes who had excelled themselves in wars and other adventures in the history of the *Du* and as a result were co-opted into the Council of *Fiahawo*.

The selection of an Ewe *Dufiagã* was not linked with any economic interests of the electors. The *Zikpuitɔ*, i.e. the stool father of the royal lineage, nominated the candidate he considered most suitable; his nomination was subject to the approval of *Dumegãwo*. The nomination process was highly confidential and only a handful of members of the council of *Dumegãwo* were informed. Even the candidate nominated should not be hinted in any way. The candidate had to fulfil some conditions, namely:

1. He should not be left-handed. It was unbecoming for an Ewe chief to gesticulate with his left hand while speaking.
2. The candidate, in the words of Manoukian, "should be at least pre-possessing enough not to be a laughing stock to neighbouring sub-tribes".[17]
3. He must be intelligent and morally strong.

The approved candidate was grabbed and installed, whether or not he was interested in the position. The selection of sub-chiefs and other members of *Fiahawo* was more or less similar to that of the *Dufiagã*.

---

[16] The royal lineage of Gbedzigbe Hohoe comprised three sub-lineages, namely the Adom, Kadrake and Asamani. The *royal sib* of Anlo consisted of two maximal lineages: Adzoviawo and Bate.

[17] Manoukian, M., 1952, p. 32.

Functions of Dufiagā

The *Dufiagā* was the highest political authority within the *Du*. He presided over the councils of *Fiahawo* and *Dumegāwo*, as well as over the supreme court of the *Du*. As the representative of the ancestors and the living subjects of the *Du* the *Dufiagā* had to mediate between the former and the latter. The organization and supervision of important festivals and rituals was also his responsibility. A most important task of the paramount chief was to periodically sacrifice to the *Fiazikpui*.[18] With the help of his sub-chiefs, the *Sohefia* and lineage elders the *Dufiagā* had to organize regular communal labour for the construction and maintenance of roads, markets, etc.

His Privileges

There were no standardized privileges for Ewe chiefs. In the interior the paramount chiefs exacted no regular tributes apart from specific parts of every leopard, lion and elephant killed. Voluntary work by subjects for the chief was common. Regular tributes seemed, however, to constitute a substantial part of royal revenue on the coast. According to Westermann all traders, farmers and hunters must regularly give the king of Glidzi merchandised goods, meat and other foodstuffs. He claims that 50 per cent of soap produced by any woman found its way to the household of the Glidzi king. All able-bodied subjects of Glidzi were also expected to work at least once on the king's farms during each farming season without pay. They were, however, fed during their engagement.[19]

The slave trade was another lucrative source of revenue for the coastal Ewe chiefs. While most of the slaves were sold to European slavers directly by the chiefs, a certain number was normally reserved as agricultural labour force.[20]

Court fees and fines were part of the royal income. The king of Glidzi received 50 per cent of the court revenue.[21] Half of the rest (i.e. 25 per cent) went to his chief *Asafohene*; the deputy *Asafohene* received one-quarter of the remaining 25 per cent. The rest of the money went to the royal treasury.[22]

Westermann's claim creates the impression that the court fees and fines were shared only by a small circle within the king's

---

[18] The *Fiazikpui*. a small stool owned and worshipped by each chief was according to Ewe belief, the embodiment of strength and power of the dead and the living subjects of the *Du*. The dead were permanently represented by a council of ancestor spirits, who were always in the close vicinity of the *Fiazikpui*.
Each sub-unit of the *Du* (i.e. each village, each lineage, etc.) had a *Fiazikpui* whose status corresponded to the status of its head in the power hierarchy of the Du. The *Fiazikpui* of the *Dufiagu* was, therefore, the supreme stool.
[19] Westermann, D., 1935 pp. 228–230.
[20] *Op. cit.*
[21] *Op. cit.*
[22] *Op. cit.*, p. 228

executive council. One wonders if this pattern of sharing was acceptable to other officers of the court whose functions could not be said to be irrelevant.

Westermann identifies another form of sharing court revenue among other Ewe groups. According to him the paramount chief received one third. One-third was shared by the rest of the executive council while the remaining one-third went to the *Du* treasury.[23] Chiefs received yearly tributes from aliens resident in their territory.[24]

Westermann is of the opinion that the above-named income sources were not of any great significance, for the chiefs very often had to depend on the financial support of their kinship units, especially during great receptions and celebrations.[25] Westermann's assessment would have been more helpful if he had measured the functions of the ruling organs against the income and tributes in kind they periodically received. Knowledge of the relevance of their administrative activity to production and therefore to the development of the forces of production would have helped us correctly assess the essence of the surplus they enjoyed.

Officers of *Dufiagā*

There were slight differences in the structure and size of the executive councils of the various Ewe paramount chiefs. A common feature was the unique position of the sub-chiefs, (i.e. chiefs of the various Gbɔtawo constituting a *Du*) as the most senior officers of the *Dufiagā*. Other important office holders were the *Agbonugla* (among the Anlo and Glidzi) and *Zikpuitɔ* (inland Ewe). The former was the oldest male member of the royal lineage. He was the president of the executive council and mediator between the elders and the king. The latter was the stool father and senior adviser to the *Dufiagā*. He could recommend the destoolment of the *Dufiagā* if he *(Zikpuitɔ)* was no longer satisfied with him. It was not befitting for an Ewe chief to speak loudly in public; the *Tsyiame* must repeat almost every formal pronouncement the chief made in public or at receptions in his residence.[26] He was the mouth-piece of the council of *Fiahawo* and had to lead almost every delegation sent to other *Duwo* by both the *Fiahawo* and *Dumegāwo*. Every major kinship unit *(kɔ)* among the inland Ewe had an *Asafohene* (chief warrior) who in times of war served as the commanding officer of his unit. In peace time he helped the council of lineage elders in keeping law and order. In some *Duwo* the senior *Asafohene* was next in authority to the sub-chiefs; the *Avadada* in Anlo was the equivalent of the senior *Asafohene*. Both of them were the supreme commanders of the warriors[27] and all lineage *Asafohenewo* and *Gawo* were subordinate to them. The *Gawo* (*ga* = singular) in Anlo

---

[23] *Op. cit.*
[24] *Op. cit.*, p. 229.
[25] *Op. cit.*
[26] The motive behind this tradition is to conceal possible slips of tongue by the chief which could expose him to ridicule. The *Tsyiame* was usually very eloquent.
[27] Wars were waged to avenge aggression, to defend, to punish, to gain

were the junior *Avadadawo* who commanded warriors in wars. In peace time they assumed the role of police officers. In some other *Duwo* the senior *Asafohene* was subordinate to the *Sɔhefia* who was the next in the power hierarchy to the sub-chiefs. The *Sɔhefia*, leader of the commoners, was very influential and fearful. He could initiate and carry through the destoolment of the *Dufiagā* and any of his officers. His source of power was the rank and file of the population of a *Du*. He mediated between the chiefs and the mass of the common people. The *Sɔhefia* organized communal work, settled disputes and imposed punishment in specified cases. His main job was to jealously protect and defend the interests of the common people against possible encroachments by the nobility, as well as to check chiefs who were becoming too independent in decision-making. Surprisingly his office was also hereditary.

Other officers of the *Dufiagā*, usually found in the coastal areas, were *Wuga* (keeper of royal canoes and boats), *Asiga* (market overseer), *Tɔga* (custodian of rivers), *Agboga* (porter), *Wuga* (keeper of drums), *Fiagbɔvi* (personal servant of the chief/king), *Xɔnuvi* (royal manciple). *Asonfowo* (body guards) and *Ametatsolawo* (executioners) were indispensable officers of every Ewe paramount chief/king.

Every *Tefia* (sub-chief) had similar officers though less in number. In most cases the *Ametatsolawo* (executioners) in the various villages of a *Du* were under the direct control of the *Dufiaga*.

All executive and administrative political officials, including the paramount chiefs, worked part-time. Put differently: there was no separation of mental labour from physical labour like in Notsie.

The Legal System[28]

The pre-colonial Ewe law was not codified; it was a law in the sense of "social control through the systematic application of the force of politically organized society."[29]

The pre-colonial Ewe political structure, as has been pointed out above, was characterized, among other things, by the existence of hierarchically organized executive and administrative organs, whose functions were controlled and directed by laid-down legal and ethical normative principles. The fairly elaborate legal system of the pre-colonial Ewe owed its existence partly to the nascent socio-economic inequalities that characterized the various Ewe communities especially in the coastal areas. These inequalities gave rise to rudimentary development of social classes and its accompanying contradictions. To regularize the gradually developing conflict loaded human relations a legal machinery was evolved gradually by the privileged social strata. This process, rooted in Ketu and

territory, to plunder. Several intra-Ewe and inter-ethnic wars of this kind were waged in the post-Notsie era. The Taviefe-Ziavi wars, the Ho-Peki wars, the Peki-Taviefe wars, the Ewe-Ashanti wars, the Ewe-Akwamu wars, etc. were typical examples.

[28] Our discussion of the Ewe legal system is based partly on the works of Schelettwein, A., 1930, p. 13 ff. and Westermann, D., p. 260 ff.

[29] Rescue, P. (quoted by D. Tait, 1961, p. 61).

Notsie traditions, was accelerated in the post-Notsie period by the fairly rapid development of the forces of production that occurred in this period.

The Ewe clearly differentiated crimes from civil offences. Murder, manslaughter, bodily harm, robbery, sorcery, witchcraft, character assassination, extortion were regarded as serious crimes. Capital punishment was imposed all over on anybody found guilty of murder or treason. Spiritual murderers were exiled in some *Duwo* while capital punishment was imposed on them in others. The method a murderer used in killing his victim cou'd be used in his execution. In Glidzi, burglars were chained and beaten up for several months.[30] Embezzlement of public funds, extortion and assault, were punishable by fines. Fines were also imposed on people found guilty of offences such as adultery, insults, hooliganism, etc. All circumstances leading to the commission of suicide were subject to a thorough investigation and anybody whose actions directly or indirectly contributed to the incident was heavily fined.

An aspect of the Ewe law which clearly reflected the contradictions generated by the sanctioned pattern of surplus appropriation was the well-defined property law. This law safe-guarded the right of the individual to own slaves, to exploit bondsmen and own privately important means of production, such as nets, boats, canoes, cattle herds, fishing grounds in the lagoons, and to some extent, land.

Due to the rapid economic development in the coastal areas (partly caused by commercial contacts with European traders) land quickly acquired commercial value here and there and shortly before formal colonial rule plots of land were being sold or leased. Inland, land was only sold when a lineage or clan was in debt or had to pay tributes imposed as a result of war. According to the paramount chief of Klefe[31] several lineages in Klefe had to sell land to be able to pay tributes to the king of Akwamu during the Akwamu occupation of western Ewe-land in 1820–1883. Private ownership of land was, however, uncommon in the interior. Generally, land was owned collectively on kinship unit basis. Members of a lineage short of land were offered land on a temporary basis by other lineages having more than enough for cultivation. As a token of gratitude the recipients presented the head of the giver lineage with minor gifts such as palmwine or food-stuffs.

The Ewe believed that the land was jointly owned by both the living and the dead members of the community. The land could not therefore be leased or sold by individuals. Land could be sold only by the lineage as a whole if the latter was hard-pressed economically and by means of sacrifice appeased the ancestors. After some generations, privately owned land became lineage property because of the growing number of descendants of the original owner.

Family Law

Traditional Ewe society allowed monogamous and polygynous

[30] Schlettwein, M., 1930. p. 108.
[31] Togbe Afele Dzaga X.

forms of marriage. Polyandry, levirate and sororate marriages were not practised. Bride-price, though indispensable, was not a significant means of wealth accumulation. Adultery was punishable by fines, and divorce was permitted. A guilty wife in a divorce case had to pay back a sum of money equal to the total cost of all that the husband had provided her with during the time of their marriage. If vice versa, the man had to compensate the woman with a sum of money fixed by the court trying the case.

The position of the woman in marriage was subordinate to that of her husband. In coastal areas wives had to kneel down when handing out things to their husbands. The Ewe woman, however, enjoyed economic independence which was legally and morally sanctioned by tradition.

In the polygynous family the woman who had been married first was, irrespective of her age, the most senior. If, however, a child of a junior wife happened to be the oldest son of the husband then he (son) became the heir of his father irrespective of the subordinate position of his mother vis-à-vis the first wife.

Inheritance Law

The dominance of patriarchal authority among the pre-colonial Ewe was reflected in the inheritance law. As indicated above the first-born son was the sole heir of his father. He was, however, morally obliged to hand out part of the inherited property to his sisters and younger brothers. In case the brothers and sisters were under age he had to cater for them till they became mature enough to manage their share of the property. The widow of the dead had no claim to the property left behind by her husband.

The Anlo and Glidzi allowed some form of matrilineal inheritance. The limited acceptance of it is explained by a historical episode. The Anlo, it is said, forgot their royal stool in tyranny-stricken Notsie during their escape. A nephew of Togbe Sri,[32] the Paramount chief of Anlo, went back to Notsie and safely brought the stool when Sri's own son refused, on the advice of his mother (Sri's wife), to do so. Since then descendants of both Sri and his sister have been ruling the Anlo nation alternately. This new royal matrilineal authority soon spread beyond the royal house and became a common tradition in the whole of Anlo and neighbouring *Duwo*.

In Glidzi, children could only claim the farms and private land of their deceased father. All other property, such as clothes, money, livestock, boats, nets, slaves and other valuable objects went to the sons of the sisters of the dead man.

Executive Organs

The executive organs of a *Du* were the *Fiahawo* of the sub-chiefs and the paramount chief, and the executive council of the *Sohewo*. All of them could try cases and impose punishment on those found

[32] Son of one of Sri's sisters.

guilty. Within each kinship unit lineage elders also settled disputes. Serious conflicts and disputes not successfully settled by lineage elders were referred to the court of the sub-chief. Unsatisfied plaintiffs and accused could apply to the court of the *Dufiagā* for deliverance from the decision of the court of the sub-chief.

In Anlo and Glidzi, where in each case several *Duwo* were centrally administered by a king, the latter's court was the highest court of appeal. Serious crimes such as murder, treason, man-slaughter, homicide were tried by the king's court. Arrests, punishments, flogging, etc. were carried out by the *Asonfowo* and *Ameta-tsolawo*.

Religion

Religious beliefs and sanctions constituted part of the socio-political power structure of pre-colonial Ewe society. They were effective super-structural traits which in no small measure protected the sanctioned material position of the emerging privileged social groups.

Besides ancestor worship and the activities of *Yewe* and *Vudu* secret societies, there were three clearly identified groups of gods and two important categories of magical art.[33] The first two groups of gods, i.e. the sky and earthly gods were headed by *Mawu*, the most senior sky god. *Mawu* was the creator of the universe and mankind. The Ewe believe that he was originally in close physical proximity with man, but human beings became so polluted with sins that *Mawu* had to retreat to an endless distance keeping away completely out of touch. Everything positive and good emanated from *Mawu*. This great god was so kind to mankind that he sent rains to the earth to make cultivation of crops possible. He had a human shape and was always clothed in a sparkling, white robe.

In the nearest proximity of *Mawu* were always two gods called Sogble and Sodza. Sodza, the eldest son of *Mawu*, was usually sent by his father to earth in the form of dreadful thunder and inflamed lightning to punish wrong-doers. Sogble, the female counter-part of Sodza, appeared as a pleasant luminous lightning accompanied by gently rolling thunder. Whenever Sodza roared and threatened to strike she intervened pleading for clemency.

The *Trɔwo* were earthly gods. Their dwelling places were mountains, rocky slopes, gullies, caves, big trees, rivers, fountains, etc. *Trɔ* was supposed to mediate between mankind and *Mawu*. *Trɔwo* imposed punishment in the form of violent storms, drought and diseases. They could be ordered by *Mawu* or invoked by any individual to kill an offender. *Miano*, a goddess, was the head of the earthly gods. She was regarded as the wife of *Mawu* to whom she was subordinate in terms of power. *Miano* played a decisive role in the creation of plants, animals and other earthly gods. She was the source of nourishment for all living things.

See (1) Spieth, J., 1906, pp. 62–74.
     (2) Asamoa, A., 1971, pp. 214–216.

32

The tutelary gods, believed to shape the destiny of every human being, were the third category of gods. Their permanent abode was *Amedzɔfe*, home of the spirits. The tutelary gods were always in the company of human beings, directing the activities of every person in consonance with his/her laid-down *Gbetsi*, i.e. destiny. Everybody's *Gbetsi* was believed to be always in *Amedzɔfe. Dzɔgbe, Kpegbonɔla, Aklama* were some of the tutelary spirits, which apart from their role mentioned earlier, protected each individual human being against any possible form of non-predestined death.

The Ewe differentiated magic in private life from magic in the social domain. Magic in private life was a means of self defence against sorcery, witchcraft and other evil spirits. Magic in the social terms was a variety of trials by ordeal . The *Aka* (ordeal) was usually staged whenever a chief's court could not by normal legal means pass judgment because of lack of evidence. One type of *aka* was particularly dreadful, if not cruel. The *aka* magician poured boiling oil into the palms of the candidates assembled for trial. He could even ask them to drink the boiling oil. The hand or mouth of the guilty person got terribly burnt. It is said that innocent candidates normally went through the same ordeal unharmed.

During another type of trial by ordeal the accused persons, each holding high a healthy chicken (bought by him-/her-self), were asked one by one to let go the chicken. Each accused was asked to say that his/her chicken should die on the spot if he/she was guilty of the offence or crime they had been accused of. After this pronouncement, it is said, the chicken of the guilty died immediately, while those of the innocent just walked off.

Ancestor worship, closely connected with the belief in life-after death, played a significant role in the religious life of the Ewe. Like other Africans, the Ewe believed that they were always in close contact with the spirits of their ancestors, who controlled their activities and protected them against evil spirits, accidents and calamities. The belief that the ancestors could impose punishments was also widespread. To forestall possible punitive actions by the ancestors, sacrifices were periodically made.

33

PART III

THEORETICAL APPRAISAL

Introduction

Attempts have been made by both Marxists and non-Marxists to classify traditional African societies. A good example of non-Marxist contributions in this field of scientific inquiry is *African Political* Systems edited by Evans-Pritchard and Fortes.

Usually regarded in reactionary, conservative, anthropological sociological circles in Africa as a masterpiece, the classification model leaves much to be desired. The structural and functional dimensions of the political institutions mainly used as classification criteria do not and cannot throw any clear light on the qualitative contents of the various socio-economic formations on the continent. What is meant here is that the classification model hinges almost exclusively on the functional and structural dimensions of selected superstructural traits. Thus the mechanism of PF–PR relationship,[1] its intercourse with super-structural categories a process instrumental in the qualitative transformation of society, is not considered as a vital classification criterion. Attempts made here and there in the book by individual contributors to consider economic issues are restricted to a mere enumeration of economic branches and material privileges of the ruling aristocracies. No analysis of the general mode of production in which the material privileges of the administrative machinery (e.g. tributes and court fees) are rooted is made. Thus the main, if not the only criterion determining the classification is whether or not a political system is centrally or acephalously organized. And even the examination of the various societies within this limited classification framework is done only in a synchronic perspective. Thus vital diachronic processes which have been and are partly instrumental in shaping the essence of the political structure are ignored. The net result of this deficient methodological approach is that African traditional political systems which are qualitatively simi'ar are regarded as different in essence and those diverse in quality are thrown into the same category of identity.

It is fairly easy to differentiate qualitatively a hunting and gathering horde from an agricultura! community. But if it comes to comparing more complex social systems difficulties arise, calling for great caution. For example, the Ibo of Nigeria "had more

[1] P.F.—Productive Forces.
[1] P.R.—Production Relations.

than two hundred autonomous, self-contained groups"[2] without any central authority while similar political groups, though semi-autonomous in terms of political power, constituting the Oyo Empire, accepted a central power embodied in the King in Oyo. An analysis of the sub- and super-structural categories of the two ethnic groups (Ibo and Yoruba) would reveal a striking identity in their socio-economic formations. Both societies had, for instance, almost the same level of economic development and similar production relations.

The absence of a centralized administrative machinery among the Ibo people needs not imply administrative simplicity. Ottenburg's examination of the Afikpo Ibo clearly shows "how the integration of Ibo society is achieved by the interplay of many elements, especially a strong development of associations — a culture trait that is characteristic of West Africa as a whole. Associations that play a part in integrating Afikpo Society take many forms: age grades, a village men's society, title societies . . ."[3], secret organizations, such as the fearful Ogo Society and Oracle institutions. Thus, the Ibo recognized super-structural institutions which, cutting across village boundaries, not only maintained Ibo identity and unity but also protected the statuses and interests of materially and socially privileged individua's and groups in Ibo society.

Similar super-structural institutions were in existence in the Yoruba Kingdom besides centralized authority. Therefore if broadly seen in historical materialist context, the Ibo and Yoruba cannot be said to have qualitatively different socio-economic formations. Of course the central administration in Oyo, through the mechanisms of its surplus appropriation, was generating quantitative modifications which might eventually negate the quality of the Yoruba Society. For instance, the notorious raids of plunder staged by the Oyo Empire against her weaker neighbours could have eventually transformed the Yoruba Society into a slave formation if the Oyo aristocracy had taken captives and made their labour the basis of production. The same aristocracy might also have been forced by multiplying internal contradictions connected with the raids to enserf the free Yoruba peasantry by seizing all land and distributing it among its vassals. It is mainly in this light that the existence of centralized authority among the Yoruba could be said to be particularly interesting. But we should not lose sight of the possibility that a similar political situation could also develop among the Ibo. The village council of elders and other organized groups wie'ding social and political power in the village could eventually enserf their fellow free peasants, should this development be historically inevitable.

Our discussions so far have, no doubt, strengthened our position that it is impossible to follow the objective, dynamic functional dimensions of super-structural institutions without understanding their economic contents or roots.

Attempts by marxists to identify the production relations of tradi-

---

[2] Ottenberg, P., 1965, p. 1.
[3] *Op. cit.*
[4] *Op. cit.*, p. 3 ff.

4

tional African societies have often run into difficulty, if not confusion, partly because of inadequate knowledge in African socio-cultural history. Thus, it is quite common to see Marxist scholars ascribing false socio-economic formations to African communities. The tendency very often is to depict them as feudal.[5] Another question which occupies Marxists in their general debate on pre-capitalist socio-economic formations is whether or not Marx's concept of Asiatic Mode of Production (AMP) is applicable to non-Asiatic societies. The general consensus now seems to be that the term should not be restricted to Asia. Marxists therefore do not hesitate to attach the AMP label to traditional African societies.[6] Meanwhile, let us come back to the problem of feudalism.

The term feudalism denotes the unique quality of a specific socio-economic formation. A mode of production can be described as feudal only after cumulative processes have negated the qualitative definiteness of the socio-economic formation within whose bosom the new feudal quality has emerged. It is the qualitative uniqueness of a mode of production that differentiates it from other socio-economic formations; in other words, it is by virtue of this essential definiteness that it is the given social system. When, therefore, we accept the scientific term, feudalism, as reflecting the quality or essence of a socio-economic system then it is obvious that the qualitative content of the latter cannot be reduced to its separate properties, since it embraces and is inseparable from the whole social system. If in the light of this argument, we depict an African social system as feudal, then possible differences between a European and the African feudal formations could only be insignificantly quantitative and not qualitative notwithstanding the European origin of the term "Feudalism".

Not seldom do we, in our haste to identify feudalism here and there on the African continent at all costs, miserably fail, when assessing African communities, to correctly relate cumulative processes to the qualitative transformations they generate and vice versa. We are, thus, unable to observe the magnitudes and scopes of the development of external properties and of course, the limit these quantitative changes reach before they negate the quality of the old social order. Our failure, if not inability, to do this makes us to jump to embarrassing conclusions, such as that pre-colonial Monomotapa, Zulu, Yoruba, Ashanti and other Akan societies, Matabele, etc. were feudal just because we see in each of these polities one or two questionable feudal traits.[7] Prah argues, in support of his claim that the Akan were feudal, that "the word akoa means 'vasal', 'client', or 'subjects' as distinct from odonko meaning slave. A sub-chief could be an akoa or a paramount chief, and the sub-chief himself had his own nkoa. . .The late pre-capitalist

[5] See (a) Protechin, I., 1960.
        (b) Prah, K., 1976.
[6] See (a) Chesneaux, J., 1969, p. 36 ff.
        (b) Godelier, M., 1969, p. 87.
        (c) Suret-Canale J., 1966, p. 108 ff.
[7] See (a) Prah, K., 1976, p. 45.
        (b) Rattray, R., 1929 p. 102 ff. (Rattray was no marxist).
        (c) Potechin, I., 1961.

Ashanti aristocracy, although not estate-owing in a highly individualized and particularized sense as we know it today, still operated landed holdings with the labour of slaves and serfs, and extracted tributes and taxes from their social inferiors and their conquered client states. This system of tribute and tax extraction was carried up the Pyramid of aristocratic positions and office."[8] Prah does not provide us with any further evidence in support of his feudalism.

One would have expected him to have at least examined in detail one of his several feudal states in Africa clearly identifying (1) the magnitude of slave and the so-called serf labour in relation to free, peasant labour; (2) the productivity of each labour pattern in the total system of production; (3) production relations with a special emphasis on the land tenure system and patterns of surplus appropriation; (4) sub and super-structural relationships.

Prah would then have been able to present us with a model of feudalism in Africa. We would fully agree with Prah that "Labour being the source of all value and all wealth," is the crucial factor in any economic system" and that "The expenditure and distributive patterns of labour in the creation and distribution of surpluses is thus the crucial and overriding diagnosing criterion in the analysis of economic structures."[9] But then we should note that we could identify the essence of the economic structure or mode of production under examination only when we are able to detect the dominant labour pattern and the property relations which determine its essence. A labour pattern cannot be dominant unless the property relations in which it is rooted dominate the total system of production.[10]

Prah seems to lose sight of this scientific fact. He is yet to prove with concrete data, for example (1) that in Ashanti, one of his feudal societies, the ruling aristocracy, usually including the priesthood, owned privately all land and (2) that most of the Ashanti peasants had to pay ground rent which covered the products of their surplus labour.

For us, production relations in Ashanti did not differ qualitatively from those of the Post-Notsie Ewe, though there were certainly differences in terms of external properties.[11]

Our main argument against Prah and other discoverers of feudalism in Africa is that feudalism is a socio-economic formation which could emerge within the bosom of a primitive communal or a slave-owning society. During the transformation processes new traits could appear and eventually pave the way for a full-fledged feudal

---

[8] Prah, K., 1976, p. 45.
[9] Op. cit., p. 45.
[10] On European feudalism Marx writes, "Personal dependence here characterizes the social relations of production just as much as it does the other spheres of life organized on the basis of that production. But for the very reason that personal dependence forms the ground-work of society, there is no necessity for labour and its product to assume a fantastic form different from their reality." Marx, K., Capital Vol. 1, p. 81.
[11] See (a) Asamoa, A., 1964.
  (b) Earlier chapters and conclusions of this contribution.

development. Through successive additions these traits tend to accumulate; during this process the old social order gradually disintegrates while the new feudal one takes shape. Till this process of qualitative transformation is complete the society cannot be described as feudal, in spite of external feudal properties observable in the cumulative process. The competent scientific observer must be able to distinguish between the level of overall quantitative modifications and the degree of the qualitative transformations the society is undergoing. The identification and dissection of the dominant production relations is the best yard-stick for measuring this distinction.

By our discussion of feudalism so far we do not wish to suggest that traditional Africa has never tasted feudal hegemony. We agree that Ethiopia, for example, was a typical feudal formation. We are yet, however, to be convinced as far as many other traditional African societies are concerned.[12]

Asiatic Mode of Production

We shall now discuss, in some detail, the AMP concept and its applicability to the African experience.

Karl Marx did not wake up one morning to realise that he must write *Das Kapital,* one of the greatest scientific works in human history, in order to save mankind. As a matter of fact it was at a certain stage of his efforts to discover the objective laws generating a chain of social upheavals and revolutions in a number of European countries, notably France and Germany in his time, that Marx became aware of the need to devote much of his time to the study of economics. *Das Kapital,* based on a 20-year intensive research, was the outcome of that historic decision. The work detects and explains, among other things, the root causes and effects, in a wider materialist context, of alienated human relations in capitalist societies. To have access to the diachronic depth of alienation of man in capitalism, Marx, together with Engels, did not only examine the feudal mode of production within whose bosom European capitalism was nursed but also studied extensively works on slavery and a number of pre-class communalist societies.

The results of their investigations, to be precise, their identification of the various forms of pre-capitalist property relations mankind has gone through, constitute an important insight into man's social history.

Marx/Engels' earliest attempt to periodize human history seems to be found in *The German Ideology,* written in 1845–46. Marx/Engels identify here three main forms of pre-capitalist ownership, namely, tribal ownership, ancient communal and state ownership, and feudal ownership.[13] The rather scanty exposition in the *The*

---

[12] For more information on Feudalism see:
    1. Marx/Engels 1968, p. 31 ff.
    2. Dobb, M., 1972, p. 44 ff.
    Marx, K., *Capital.* Vol. 1, p. 81. ff.
[13] Marx/Engels, 1968, p. 33 ff.

German Ideology is elaborated in the *Grundrisse* written by Marx in 1857–58, i.e. 12–13 years after *The German Ideology*, had been composed.

In the *Grundrisse* Marx pays closer attention to pre-class formations, to be specific, to the so-called Ancient classical, Asiatic and Germanic Modes of Production, clearly identifying qualitative features peculiar to each formation.

The next attempt by Marx/Engels to undertake a systematic periodization of man's social history seems to have occurred in the early eighties of the 19th Century, the time Marx and Engels got to know Lewis Morgan's *Ancient Society* and other works on primitive societies.[14] Besides these three major periodization attempts the two intellectual giants examined here and there selected socio-economic institutions of primitive societies, not to mention monographic works on selected primitive communities.[15]

The main concern of Marx/Engels all along as regards their interest in primi'ive societies seemed to be to work out a general system in terms of mankind's transition from 'he primitive to civilised conditions of life. Marx, like his friend Engels, saw in Morgan's work a valuable scientific contribution which constituted a solid basis for any genuine work of periodization. Marx's own drafted periodization outlines, descernible only through a meticulous examination of his excerpts (and comments thereon) from ethnological works of Morgan, Maine, Phear and Lubbock,[16] seem to indicate Marx's appreciation of Morgan's scheme.

Engels who saw Marx's excerpts for the first time when going through the post-humous manuscripts of Marx accepted the latter's general position on Morgan.[17]

The *Origin of The Family, Private Property* and *The State* summarizes, to a great extent, Marx/Engels' position on Morgan's *Ancient Society*. The book contains obsolete and incorrect issues,

---

[14] Krader suggests that Marx began to excerpt Morgan's work "dur'ng the winter and perhaps Spring of 1880–1881" quoting an indirect reference Marx makes to Morgan in one of his drafted letters (dated March 8, 1881) to Vera Zasulich as evidence (See Krader, L., 1972, p. 86–87). Engels, Krader claims, apparently became aware of Morgan's work in 1883–84 (*op. cit.*)

[15] See *The Holy Family*; *Anti Duehring*; *Capital* Vol I; *India Letters*; *Marx's drafted letters to Vera Zasulich*; *Die Markt* (MEW 19), etc.

[16] See Krader. L., 1972, p. 97 ff.

[17] Krader writes, "Marx worked out his system in regard to the transition of mankind from the primitive to the civilized social condition, but we can see no more than the outlines, taking as the basis of it the works that he chose for annotation and excerption, together with what is known of the sc.entific, political and historical positions of the authors and the points he raised from their works. Morgan was his chief support. Maine his opponent ... Engel accords with the position of Marx in general, but there are significant differences between them; Engels was less deep and less precise than Marx;" (*op. cit.*, pp. 81–82). Krader explains how Marx and Engels differ drawing attention at the same time to where Marx agrees and disagrees with Morgan (see *op. cit.*, p. 76 ff). See also Engels, F., 1970, p.

but these are largely factual inexactitudes, which no doubt affect abstract deductions here and there.[18]

In spite of these short-comings the scheme in *The Origin* ... is anchored totally in the Marxist materialist concept of history, and is so elastic that we find it a very useful guide in our humble attempt to identify the production relations of the Pre-colonial Ewe.

Ruben and Welskopf accuse Engels of identifying Military Democracy (coined by Morgan) with the earliest forms of classless societies including the AMP. Guhr defends Engels by pointing out that the latter's position on the AMP was very clear. In support of his notion Gurh refers to some letters and works by Engels (Engels to Marx, 26th May, 1853; 6th June 1853; Marx to Engels, 2nd June, 1853; 14th June, 1853; *Enzyklopaedie-Aufsaetze Afghanistan*, Birman; NEW 14; *Anti-Duehring*).[19] What seems to worry Engels' critics as regards the concept of Military Democracy (MD) is that while the term, the Asiatic Mode of Production, had been widely used by Marx and Engels from 1853 to 1859 *(Indienbriefe Grundrisse; Zur Kritik . . .)*; then in 1867 *(Das Kapital)* and in 1876 *(Anti-Duehring)* the AMP was dropped in subsequent works on pre-class societies by Marx and Engels which appeared between 1881 and 1892.[20]

The omission of the AMP term in the latter works by Marx and Engels is not of crucial significance as people would like us to believe. As pointed out above Marx and Engels regarded Morgan's *Ancient Society* as the most systematic comprehensive work on the periodization of man's early history at the time. Engels writes, "Morgan was the first person with expert knowledge to attempt to introduce a definite order into the pre-history of man; unless important additional material necessitates alterations, his classification may be expected to remain in force."[21]

It is therefore not unreasonable to suggest that Marx and Engels dropped the AMP term in favour of a term used by Morgan to denote a particular mode of production qualitatively identical with the AMP. Marx and Engels have not made their position clear on the issue. A close study of the *Origin* ... and the chapter on pre-capitalist modes of production in the *Grundrisse* would, however, reveal a striking qualitative identity of the concepts of *Barbarism* and AMP. In other words, Marx/Engels must have consciously dropped the AMP term in favour of *Barbarism*. Engels regards Military Democracy as the system of government characteristic of the Upper Stage of *Barbarism*. Engels does nott seem

[18] See (below), for example, pages 46–47.
[19] Guhr, K., 1969, p. 18.
    See also Engels, F., 1970, p. 571: One clearly sees here how Engels' understanding of Military Democracy is vulgarized by his critics.
[20] See (a) Guhr, K., 1969. p. 18.
    (b) *Marx's drafted letters to Vera Zasulitch.*
    (c) Engels' "Origin . : ."
[21] Engels, F., 1970, p. 461.

40

to identify the term with the whole socio-economic formation of Barbarism.[22]

Now, Ruben and Welskopf, and other Engels' critics would argue that the AMP and Barbarism are not qualitatively totally identical. They might argue that the disintegration processes reflecting the rapid class formation at the Upper Stage of *Barbarism* are absent in the AMP formation. But then we should remember that Morgan and Engels examine *Barbarism* in diachronic and synchronic perspectives; hence their division of the *barbarian* epoch into three stages while Marx's dissection of the AMP is largely synchronic though he is aware of its savage past, and even predicts an eventual negation of the AMP. That is, if Marx had had data on the transformation of an AMP community into a full class society he would have also identified the various stages of the negation of that community.[23]

In other words, we could safely liken the Upper *Barbarian* stage to the last, i.e. disintegration stage of the AMP which Marx could not consider in his work.

In spite of the intensified disintegration of the *Barbarian* formation at its upper stage of development it still remains qualitatively barbarian because the quantitative modifications occurring in the system have not yet fully substituted a new quality for the *barbarian* one.[24] But to be precise, the AMP as outlined by Marx, is in our view, not different in terms of qualitative content from the Lower and Middle Stages of *Barbarism*.

The AMP, as far as Marx is concerned, is the stage of development that follows the decay of the earliest form of communalist mode of production.[25] This does not imply that Marx expects every first primitive communalist society to go through an AMP formation. Marx points out that the emergence of the AMP does not imply that the AMP is devoid of any communalistic traits. Karl Marx pays a special attention to the AMP production relations, drawing attention to the budding antagonisms manifest in the partial appropriation of the surplus labour of the peasants by the chief or the despot. Land and irrigation technology (a common feature in Asian Communities), as the most important means of production, are held in trust for the people by what Marx calls the highest unity, that is, a council of elders representing all kinship units of the community and which is headed by a tribal chief or despot.

---

[22] *Op. cit.*, p. 571.

[23] See Marx's excellent analysis of the Asiatic, Ancient classical and Germanic forms of property. Marx, K., 1977, pp. 485–498).

[24] See Engels, J., 1970, pp: 570–71: Here Engels consistently draws attention to the gradual disintegration of Upper Barbarism. In spite of that he still refers to the people of this stage as barbarians.

[25] Marx, K., 1977 (Grundrisse), p. 472.
Marx's concept of the first communalist mode of life as outlined here seems to agree largely with Morgan's concept of savagery adopted by Engels. It agrees with my concept of palaeo-communalism.

The community is recognized as the occupants and possessors of the land, a privilege which guarantees the community members the equal right of usufruct.

The role of hydraulic technology in the AMP is an issue that generates a lot of confusion in the minds of both Marxist and non-Marxist scholars. Both Marx and Engels, no doubt, emphasize the role played by large-scale collective works connected with artificial irrigation in agriculture in the development of oriental centralised authority and despotism.[26] But nowhere have they ever suggested that a polity cannot be an Asiatic formation unless it employs irrigation technique in agriculture as some authors would like us to believe.[27] Marx ascribes the fairly high level of labour productivity, the cause of the surplus produced in the AMP formation, to the efficient, centrally planned and administered labour organization manifest in the technique of artificial irrigation. As the major criterion for classification Marx uses the essence of production relations and the quality of super-structural categories emanating from and protecting these relations.

The part of the community's surplus labour appropriated by the highest unity, that is the ruling organs, "takes the form of tribute, etc. as well as of common labour for the exaltation of the unity, partly of the real despot, partly of the imagined clan-being, the god. Now, in so far as it actually realized itself in labour, this kind of communal property can appear either in the form where the little communes vegetate independently alongside one another, and where, inside them, the individual with his family work independently on the lot assigned to them, a certain amount of labour for the communal reserves, insurance so to speak, and to meet the expences of the community as such, i.e. for war, religion, etc. This is the first occurrence of the lordly dominium in the most original sense, e.g. in the Slavonic communes, in the Rumanian, etc. Therein lies the transition to villeinage (Frondiens+, etc.); or the unity may extend to the communality of labour itself, which may be a formal

---

[26] Engels writes, "However great the number of despotisms which rose and fell in Persia and India, each was fully aware that above all it was the entrepreneur responsible for the collective maintenance of irrigation throughout the river valleys, without which no agriculture was possible there. It was reserved for the enlightened English to lose sight of this in India: they let the irrigation canals and Sluices fall into decay . . ." (Engels, 1969 p. 215, "Anti-Duehring"; See also Engels' letter to Marx of June 6, 1853).

[27] See (a) Wittfogel, K., 1970. pp. 594–595.
    (b) Guenther, R., and Schrot, F. 1963, p. 229.
    (c) Habermeyer, K., 1973, pp 123–124 Accusing Suret-Canale of having dogmatically thrown most traditional African polities into the category of Asiatic Mode of Production. Habermeyer writes, "The special quality and high development level of the agriculture productive forces, the specific socialization of labour and the role of the state in the production process are the criteria which differentiate the Asiatic formations from the African class societies." (Op. cit.). In other words, Habermeyer does not regard production relations as the decisive classificatory criterion. The quotation is a translation (by me) of the original German text.

system, as in Mexico, Peru, especially, among the early Celts, a few clans in India. The communality can, further, appear within the clan system more in a situation where the unity is represented in a chief of the clan-family, or as the relation of the patriarchs among one another. Depending on that, a more despotic or a more democratic form of this community system".[28]

This clear position of Marx on the question of surplus appropriation by the administrative aristocracy and the priesthood in the Asiatic formation does not stop scholars, including some Marxists, from vulgarizing the issue. The appropriated surplus on which the reproduction of the administrative nobility and the priests not engaged in physical labour, partly hinges, is often depicted as exploitation. Some scholars even claim that this pattern of surplus appropriation shows that the Asiatic social formation is nothing but a variation of feudalism.[29] Marx makes it clear that the appropriated surplus is utilized in two major ways, namely as "communal reserves, insurance so to speak", and for the maintenance of the nobility and the priesthood.

The separation of mental labour from physical labour and the essence of their unity, reflects a certain level of the development of the forces of production, a level which makes surplus production possible. The quality of labour productivity necessary for the surplus gain is largely acquired within the dominant pattern of labour organization which constitutes an important organic aspect of the productive forces. If, therefore, the mental labour of the ruling aristocracy invested in the labour organization is accepted as a productivity-raising factor and, for that matter, as a productive force, then it is not unjust to compensate the subject of the mental labour from the surplus funds. The question of injustice as regards the nobility's share could only arise, if there is a marked qualitative and quantitative difference in the sharing system in favour of the administrative hierarchy, that is, if what goes to them is not commensurate with the quality and usefulness of their discharged mental labour. The part of surplus enjoyed by the priesthood has to be examined in the same light. Their magico-religious role is not directly productive, but certainly it is a vital fountain of spiritual satisfaction of the community. Spiritual health is a productivity raising factor, especially if we take into consideration the level of consciousness of the producers in that historical epoch. In other words, the activities of the Asiatic religious leaders are not dysfunctional, if related to production. But here again the assessment of their surplus consumption must relate

[28] Marx, K., Grundrisse, 1977, p. 473.
[29] (a) Guenther, R. and Schrott, G., p. 230.
    (b) Needham, J., 1954, pp. 103 and 139, quoted by Oscar Lange, 1963, p. 29.
    (c) Early Soviet AMP discussions, especially the *Bolshaya Sovietskaya Enciklodepia*, 1936, Vol. 32 pp. 530 and 538, quoted by Oscar Lange, *op. cit.*

to the scope of the objective usefulness of their role in the community.[30]

There is no doubt that here and there, now and then, the mental labour contributors would consume more than they deserve; and this could be easily routinized if the volume of surplus is increased through further development of the forces of production. Marx is aware of this, that is why he sees in the phenomenon the possible "transition to villeinage (Frondienst), etc."[31]

The misunderstanding of the essence of the highest unity's relation to land and how the content of this relation appertains to the aristocracy's appropriation of surplus make some writers to jump to the false conclusion that the Asiatic formation is either a feudal class society or an emerging slave mode of production.[32] Marx writes, ". . . it is not in the least a contradiction to it that, as in most of the Asiatic land-forms, the comprehensive unity standing above all these little communities appears as the higher proprietor or as the sole proprietor; the real communities hence only as hereditary possessors. Because the unity is the real proprietor and the real presupposition of communal property, it follows that this unity can appear as a particular entity above the many real particular communities, where the individual is then in fact propertyless, or, property—i.e. the relation of the individual to the natural conditions of labour and of reproduction as belonging to him, as the objective nature-given inorganic body of his subjectivity—appears mediated for him through a cession by the total unity—a unity realized in the form of the despot, the father of the many communities—to the individual, through the mediation of the particular commune. The surplus product—which is, incidentally, determined by law in consequence of the real appropriation through labour—thereby automatically belongs to this highest unity".[33]

With this statement Marx does not minimize the role of the jealously protected primitive democracy to which even the highest unity must bow in the Asiatic formation. The statement simply implies that the community land which Marx calls "the great workshop, the arsenal which furnishes both means and material of labour, as well as the seat, the base of the community", is owned by the community itself for itself through a symbolic figure, a despot, whose source of power is the community which again regulates and controls the dissemination of both economic and political power by the despot.

Our rejection of the notion that the Asiatic formation is either

[30] It seems scholars who attach the feudal label to non-feudal communities in Africa and elsewhere misunderstand the functional dimensions of surplus appropriation in those communities. They might overcome this difficulty by studying Marx's concept of the AMP more closely.
[31] See our quotation above (pp. 42–43).
[32] See (a) Ostrovitionov, K., 1945, pp: 46–49: (quoted by Oscar Lange, 1963.) (pp 2–29).
    (b) Guenther, R., and Schrott, G., p. 220.
[33] Marx, K., (Grundrisse), 1977, pp. 472–73.
See above our discussion on the use of the appropriated surplus product.

a feudal or slave formation does not imply a rejection of social contradictions in the AMP. We are aware of the organized slave labour in Ancient Egypt, Mesopotamia, Persia, China, India, etc. Although slavery was a common phenomenon in these Asiatic societies, slave labour did not constitute the general basis of production. Slave labour was employed mainly in public constructional works, such as building of pyramids, cultural centres, chapels, canals and reservoirs, tombs, etc. In other words, the reproduction mechanisms were rooted in the labour of free peasants who were in the majority. "The fundamental condition of property resting on the clan system (into which the community originally resolves itself)", Marx writes, "—to be a member of the clan—makes the clan conquered by another clan propertyless and throws it among the inorganic conditions of the conqueror's reproduction, to which the conquering community relates as its own. Slavery and serfdom are, thus, only further developments of the form of property resting on the clan system. They necessarily modify all the latter's forms. They can do this least of all in the Asiatic form. In the self-sustaining unity of Manufacture and Agriculture, on which this form rests, conquest is not so necessary a condition as where Landed Property, Agriculture are exclusively predominant. On the other hand, since in this form the individual never becomes a proprietor but only a possessor, he is at bottom himself the property, the slave of him in whom the unity of the commune exists, and slavery here neither suspends the conditions of labour nor modifies the essential relations."[34]

We have taken the trouble to discuss aspects of the AMP concept because we want to prove our claim that AMP is essentially identical with Barbarism. An examination of the Barbarism concept would also be necessary in spite of its clear exposition by Engels in the Origin . . .

Barbarism

Using Lewis Morgan's Classification Scheme, Frederick Engels identifies three main epochs of man's historical development, namely Savagery, Barbarism and Civilization. Just like Morgan, Engels sub-divides the first two epochs into a lower, middle and upper stages "according to the progress made in the production of means of subsistence"[35] and how it relates to the distribution of the products of labour.

Savagery

Lower Stage

The lower and middle stages of savagery saw the earliest and most primitive mode of production in human history. At the lower stage men lived exclusively on wild fruits, tubers, vegetables

[34] Op. cit., p. 473.
This quotation reminds us of our misgivings about Kwesi Prah's allegation that Pre-colonial Ashanti was feudal.
[35] Engels, F., 1970, p. 461.

45

which they gathered. Man was still restricted to the tropical and sub-tropical forests regarded by anthropologists and archaeologists as his original habitat. Trees served him partially as a dwelling. Articulate speech, which Engels regards as the main achievement of the epoch, was already developed. "None of the peoples that became known during the historical period", Engels writes, "were any longer in this primeval state. Although this period may have lasted for many thousands of years we have no direct evidence of its existence; but once we admit the descent of man from the animal kingdom the acceptance of this transitional stage is inevitable."[36]

Middle Stage

At the middle stage of Savagery fire was discovered and food acquisition extended to small aquatic animals, such as fish, crabs, shell fish, etc. By searching for these equatic animals man spread along river banks over other areas of the earth. Crude palaeolithic implements predominated, while the employment of the club and the spear as hunting weapons (Engels regards them as the first weapons) added game occasionally to diet. Baking pits, fish and fire were complementary discoveries of the time. "Exclusively hunting peoples, such as figure in books, that is, peoples subsisting solely by hunting, have never existed, for the fruits of the chase are much too precious to make that possible".[37] The main deduction we could safely make here is that, gathering food items was still the dominant economic activity. Engels regards the indigenous Australians and Polynesians as middle stage savages. Later ethnological discoveries, however, suggest a higher level of development of the Australians and Polynesians.[38]

Upper Savagery

The invention of the bow and arrow, "whereby wild game became a regular item of food, and hunting one of the normal occupations . . ." marks the beginning of the Upper Stage of Savagery. Engels posits that the invention of the bow and arrow which constitute a very composite instrument "presupposes long accumulated experience and sharpened mental powers, and consequently a simultaneous acquaintance with a host of other inventions."[39] First traces of settlement in villages, a limited appearance of means of production such as wooden vessels and utensils, baskets, neolithic tools, dug-out canoes, "timber and planks for house-building", etc. were the main material culture traits. "The bow and arrow", says Engels, "was for savagery what the iron sword was for barbarism and fire-arms for civilization, namely, the decisive weapon."[40]

[36] *Op. cit.*
[37] *Op. cit.*, p. 462.
[38] See Sellnow, 1, 1961, p. 209 ff.
[39] Engels, F., 1972, p. 462.
[40] *Op. cit.*

The main proposition here is that (1) the economy of Upper Savagery was, to a limited extent, diversified (i.e. it was a combination of hunting, gathering, fishing and crude handicrafts) and (2) that a rudimentary development of sedentary life was in progress.

The proposition implies that trade and domestication of plants and animals were not practised during the Upper Stage of Savagery. And since these branches of economic activity were also not known in the earlier stages of savagery we could propose, that for Morgan and Engels all *Wildbeuter*[41] were savages, since both of them are silent over the production relations of savagery. By classifying the Indians of the North-West Coast of America as Upper Savages, Engels seems to use the category of Productive Forces only as a classification criterion. It is not easy to guess why Engels, like Morgan, uses "the progress made in the production of the means of subsistence" as the only classification criterion for savagery although he has overhauled most of the economic arguments put forward by Morgan[42] and uses consistently production relations as the decisive classification criterion while examining Barbarism and the emergence of civilization.

Lack of data on the production relations of the *Wildbeuter* at the time the *Origin* . . . was written could have limited his efforts in that direction. He could also have ruled out the possibility that surplus could be produced and classes consequently emerge in a *Wildbeuter* community as confirmed by 20th Century anthropological investigations. In fact, enthnological studies on the Indians of the North-West Coast of North America have revealed a more complicated social set-up with rudimentary class antagonisms symptomatic of upper barbarian production relations.

Though Engels does not discuss the production relations of savagery, the vast literature today on the majority of the *Wildbeuter* known to History, give some idea of what, at least, upper savage production relations could have been. Thus we know today (1) that several hunting and gathering and fishing communities owned their hunting and fishing grounds collectively; (2) that they scarcely acquired surplus foodstuffs and (3) that they equally shared all the foodstuffs they acquired daily. In other words, the distribution of the collectively acquired food items was always in consonance with the delicately balanced mechanism of the group's reproduction, a tradition which ruled out contradictions between the forces and relations of production. This consciously institutionalised praxis reflected a level of super-structural organization not dreamt of in terms of quality in the period of lower savagery.

---

[41] A German umbrella name for hunters and gatherers, primitive fishing communities and harvesters.
[42] See Sellnov's brilliant critique of some of Morgan's classification criteria (Sellnov, Berlin 1961).

Savagery-super-structure

Parallel to the primitiveness of the material base of savagery was the simplicity that characterized the super-structure of the latter.[43] Conscious political organization which apparently emerged for the first time in Upper Savagery was rudimentary and structurally identical with kinship structure. Absence of classes, of state and political authority,[44] made possible by low productivity level (which was a brake on the development of social division of labour, etc.) were other superstructural features of Middle and Upper Savagery.

Barbarism

As pointed out earlier Engels divides the periods of barbarism into 3 stages (Lower, Middle and Upper Stages). "The characteristic feature of the period of barbarism", Engels writes, "is the domestication and breeding of animals and the cultivation of plants. Now the Eastern Continent, the so-called Old World, contained almost all the animals suitable for domestication and all the cultivable cereals with one exception; while the Western America, contained only one domesticable mammal, the llama, and this only in a part of the South; and only one cereal fit for cultivation, but that the best, maize. The effect of these different natural conditions was that from now on the population of each hemisphere went its own special way, and the landmarks on the border lines between the various stages are different in each of the two cases".[45]

Engels then identifies outstanding techno-economic features characteristic of each of the three barbarian stages. Thus while Lower Barbarism dates from the introduction of pottery, Middle Barbarism begins in the East, with the domestication "of animals; in the West, with the cultivation of edible plants by means of irrigation and with the use of adobes (bricks dried in the sun) and stone for buildings."[46]

"Upper Barbarism", Engels claims, "begins with the smelting of iron ore and passes into civilization through the invention of alphabetic writing and its utilisation for literary records."[47] More progress was made during Upper Barbarism in production "than in all the previous stages put together."[48] Large-scale tillage made possible

---

[43] Engels does not discuss the super-structure of savagery. Our discussion of it is based on anthropological data.

[44] Leadership and a measure of prestige but not authority as such was certainly invested in a headman (normally the oldest in the local group) and in a council of elders or family heads to organize hunting and rituals. The headman was nothing more than a primus inter pares. Neither the headman nor any council member had the power or right to compel compliance, though his advice or/and persuasion could be tolerated. As Murdock vividly puts it, decisions vital to the welfare of the horde were reached "through discussion and informal consensus while sanctions are applied exclusively through the operation of informal mechanisms of social control". (Murdock, G., 1959, p. 33).

[45] Engels F., 1970, p. 463.

[46] Op. cit.

[47] Op. cit., p. 464.

[48] Op. cit., p. 465.

by the invention of iron plough drawn by cattle, clearing and transformation of forests into arable pasture land, unlimited increase
in subsistence and rapid population growth were the most outstanding techno-economic features of Upper Barbarism.

American Indians were, according to Engels, at the time of the
conquest, culturally lower barbarian.[49] He depicts the Pueblo Indians
of New Mexico, the Mexicans, Central Americans and Peruvians
(also American Indian agricultural peoples) as typical middle
barbarians of the West while regarding the Aryans and Semites
(mainly pastoralists) as typical middle barbarians of the East. To
Upper Barbarism "belong the Greeks of the Heroic Age, the Italian
tribes shortly before the foundation of Rome, the Germans of
Tacitus and the Normans of the days of the Vikings."[50]

Economy and Super-structure of Barbarism

Aware that technology and production, though decisive in the
development of human history, could not be used solely as classification criteria, Engels relates the productivity level of each barbarian stage to both the pattern of distribution and super-structure
peculiar to that stage.

Lower Barbarism — Economy

Citing the American Indians[51] as an example, Engels claims that
the population of Lower Barbarism, was very sparse. "It was dense
only in the habitat of the tribe, surrounded by its wide hunting
grounds and beyond these the neutral protective forest which separated it from other tribes. Division of labour was a pure and simple
but growth of nature; it existed only between the two sexes. The
men went to war, hunted, fished, provided the raw material for
food and the tools necessary for these pursuits. The women cared
for the house, and prepared food and clothing; they cooked, wove
and sowed. Each was master in his or her own field of activity; the
men in the forest, the women in the house. Each owned the tools
he or she made and used; the men, the weapons and the hunting
and fishing tackle; the women, the household goods and utensils.
The household was communistic, comprising several and often
many families. Whatever was produced and used in common was
common property: the house, the garden, the long beat. Here and
only here, then, do we find the "earned property" which jurists
and economists have falsely attributed to civilised society — last
mendacious legal pretext on which modern capitalist property
rests".[52] On the economy of the pastoral lower barbarians Engels
writes, "These pastoral tribes not only produced more articles of
food, but also a greater variety than the rest of the barbarians.
They not only had milk, milk products and meat in greater abund-
ance than the others but also skins, wool, goat's hair, and the spun
and woven fabrics, which the increasing quantities of the raw material brought into commoner use. This, for the first time made
regular exchange possible. At the preceding stages, exchange could

[49] *Op. cit.*, p. 566.
[50] *Op. cit.*, p. 565.
[51] Engels does not mention a specific American Indian group.
[52] *Op. cit.*, p. 567.

only take place occasionally; exceptional ability in the making of weapons and tools may have led to a transient division of labour. Thus, unquestionable remains of workshops for stone implements of the neolithic period have been found in many places. The artificers who developed their ability in those workshops most probably worked for the community, as the permanent handicraftsmen of the Indian gentile communities still do".[53]

Trade, according to Engels, was, in Lower Barbarism, only rudimentary and intra-tribal. Inter-tribal trade (between pastoralist and non-pastoralist communities) emerged and was consolidated as a regular institution only after pastoral life had fully assumed permanent shape. At the early stage of inter-tribal exchange trade transactions were channelled through kinship heads. Exchange between individuals later predominated gradually when, as Engels puts it, "herds began to be converted into separate property".[54] Medium of exchange at this stage was cattle. Engels claims, "Such was the necessity and rapidity with which the demand for a money commodity developed at the very beginning of commodity exchange".[55]

It may be necessary to draw attention to one implication of Engels' discussion of the sub-base of Lower Barbarism. He does not use as the major classification criterion a specific form of economy, but rather the category of production relations the essence of which he meticulously relates to the lower barbarian super-structure. In other words, a pastoral community could be lower barbarian just as an agricultural gemeinde, provided the production relations of both are essentially lower barbarian.

Superstructure of Lower Barbarism

A most important superstructural institution of Lower Barbarism was the fully developed system of kinship organization which had emerged in Middle and Upper Savagery. The kinship organization had sub-divisions, which performed well-defined functions. While the tribe, according to Engels, was in some cases the highest and largest kinship and at the same time political unit, in others it was a confederacy of consanguineally-related tribes. "This simple organization," Engels writes, "was fully adequate for the social conditions from which it sprang. It was nothing more than a peculiar natural grouping capable of smoothing out all internal conflicts likely to arise in a society organized on these lines. In the realm of the external, conflicts were settled by war, which could end in the annihilation of a tribe, but never in its subjugation. The grandeur and at the same time the limitation of the gentile order was that it found no place for rulers and ruled. In the realm of the internal there was as yet no distinction between rights and duties."[56] Blood

---

[53] *Op. cit.*, pp. 567–8.
[54] *Op. cit.*, p. 568.
The implication is that collective ownership of herds was still the normal practice, inspite of the gradual appearance of separate property.
[55] *Op. cit.*
[56] *Op. cit.*, p. 566.

revenge, participation by all and sundry in public affairs, absence of social classes were other superstructural features of Lower Barbarism.

Middle Barbarism
Economy

Complex economic activity (pastoralism, agriculture, handicraft) based on tribal collective ownership of land, constituted the material base of the middle stage of barbarism. The use and working up of metals such as copper, tin, bronze, iron, gold and silver; and the technique of the weaving loom were the most important industrial achievement of this stage. Increase in production, made possible by high labour productivity, yielded surplus products. "At the same time, it increased the amount of work that daily fell to the lot of every member of the gens or household community or single family. The addition of more labour power became desirable. This was furnished by war; captives were made slaves. Under the given general historical conditions, the first great social division of labour, by increasing the productivity of labour, that is, wealth, and enlarging the field of production, necessarily carried slavery in its wake. Out of the first great social division of labour arose the first great division of society into two classes: masters and slaves, exploiters and exploited".[57] Land was still tribal property in Middle Barbarism. It was "assigned first to the gens, which, later, in its turn distributed it to the household communities for their use, and finally to individuals; these may have had certain rights of possession, but no more.[58] Engels suggests that it was at the Middle Stage of Barbarism that "herds and flocks were converted from the common property of the tribe or gens into the property of the individual heads of families . . ."[59]

Superstructure

The gentile constitution which formed the basis of administration and the exercise of power in earlier stages, especially in Lower Barbarism of man's development, was still intact in Middle Barbarism due to the fairly low level of the development of the productive forces and the unity of the latter with production relations (in spite of rudimentary contradictions between the two) at this stage.

Upper Stage of Barbarism
Economy

Frederick Engels regards Upper Barbarism as the period in which "all civilised people passed through their Heroic Age." It saw further

---

[57] Op: cit:, p. 569. The last sentence of the quotation by no means implies that Engels regards Middle Barbarism as a slave socio-economic formation or as a well developed class society. For him the appearance of slaves is only a new quantitative phenomenon at this stage.
[58] Op. cit., p. 568.

5

development of the productive forces; iron implements and weapons dominated. Walled towns with inclosing houses of stones, very often as seats of governments; rapid increase in wealth, made possible by high labour productivity in economic branches such as crafts (weaving, metal-work, etc.), which were becoming more and more specialised and an agriculture which now added oil and wine to cereals, leguminous plants and fruits, all were new relevant economic features of this period. Economic activity at this stage was so diverse that handicrafts could separate from agriculture. "The continued increase of production and with it the increased productivity of labour enhanced the value of human labour power. Slavery, which had been a nascent and sporadic factor in the preceding stage, now became an essential part of the social system. The slaves ceased to be simply assistants, but they were now driven in scores to work in the fields and workshops.[60] The division of production into two great branches, agriculture and handicrafts, gave rise to production for exchange, the production of commodities; and with it came trade, not only in the interior and on the tribal boundaries, but also overseas. All this was still very undeveloped; the precious metals gained preference as the universal money commodity, but it was not yet minted and was exchanged merely by bare weight.

The distinction between rich and poor was added to that between freemen and slaves—with the new division came a new division of society into classes. The differences in the wealth of the various heads of families caused the old communistic household communities to break up wherever they had still been preserved; and this put an end to the common cultivation of the soil for the account of the community. The cultivated land was assigned for use to the several families, first for a limited time and later in perpetuity; the transition to complete private ownership was accomplished gradually and simultaneously . . . The individual family began to be the economic unit in society."[61]

Superstructure (Upper Barbarism)

Federation and amalgamation of kindred tribes, the merger of the tribes concerned into a single territory, the indispensably growing power of the military commander, establishment of popular assembly everywhere were important superstructural development in Upper Barbarism. Engels emphasizes the role of the military commanders at the Upper Stage of Barbarism in relation to political and economic power. He writes, "The military commander of the people . . . became an indispensable and permanent official . . . The military commander, the council and the popular assembly

---

[59] Op. cit., p. 569.
[60] It is important to note that Engels, in spite of his awareness of increased slave labour at the Upper Stage of Barbarism does not depict the latter as a slave society Engels is not unaware that slave labour never dominated production in Upper Barbarism.
[61] Engels, F., 1972, pp. 570–571.

formed the organs of the military democracy into which gentile society had developed. A military democracy—because war and organization for war were now regular functions of the life of the people. The wealth of their neighbours excited the greed of the peoples who began to regard the acquisition of wealth as one of the main purposes in life. They were barbarians: plunder appeared to them easier and even more honourable than productive work".[62]

Engels' use of the term "military democracy" does not imply the substitution of war or plunder, as a means of wealth acquisition, for production relations which he has consistently used as the main classification criterion. In other words, it is the pattern of distributing the war booty (and of course the alien labour embodied therein) that is decisive as far as war as an "economic" adventure is concerned.

Engels links the disintegration of the gentile constitution with the increased power of the military commander. "The robber wars increased the power of the supreme military commander, as well as of the sub-commanders. The customary election of successors from one family . . . was gradually transformed into hereditary succession, first tolerated, then claimed and finally usurped; the foundation of hereditary royalty and hereditary nobility was laid. In this manner the organs of the gentile constitution were gradually torn from their roots in the people, in gens, phratry and tribe, and the whole gentile order was transformed into its opposite: from an organization of tribes for the free administration of their own affairs it became an organization for plundering and oppressing their neighbours; and correspondingly its organs were transformed from instruments of the will of the people into independent organs for ruling and oppressing their own people. This could not have happened, had not the greed for wealth divided the members of the gentes into rich and poor; had not "property differences in a gens changed the community of interest into antagonisms between members of a gens" (Marx), and had not the growth of slavery already begun to brand working for a living as slavish and more ignominious than engaging in plunder."[63]

Civilization

Frederick Engels does not stop at the Upper Stage of Barbarism. He follows the gradual emergence of civilization within the bosom of the disintegrating Upper Barbarism. A crucial stage in this development is what Engels calls the threshold of civilization.

Typical economic features of this epoch are: increase and consolidation of the established divisions of labour, (between Agriculture and pastoralism, between the former and handicrafts) particularly by intensifying the contrast between town and country—with either

[62] *Op. cit.*, p. 571.
[63] *Op. cit.*, pp. 571–572. Pre-colonial Ashanti super-structure was scarcely different in essence from the Upper Barbarian super-structure Engels illustrates here. The typical Mediterranean Upper Barbarian military democracy described here reminds us of the institutionalized wars of plunder that constituted a cornerstone in the material sub-base of the Ashanti Kingdom.

of the two exercising economic supremacy over the other; the development of trade as a full time specialised economic undertaking, a development which "created a class that took no part in production, but engaged exclusively in exchanging products — the merchant,"[64] the domination of metal money as medium of exchange; land as a new source of wealth besides wealth in commodities, slaves and money; conversion of tribal land into individual hereditary property, private sale of land and discovery of mortgage;[65] "concentration and centralisation of wealth in the hands of a small class, on the one hand, and by increasing impoverishment of the masses and a growing mass of paupers, on the other" as a parallel development to "commercial expansion, money, usury, landed property and mortgage . . ."[66]

Superstructural Features

The economic contradictions characteristic of the threshold of civilization ate deeply into the gentile constitution. Territorial disintegration of kinship groups as a result of urban development which accompanied commercial expansion became rampant; new municipal administrative organs were substituted for the gentile ones, organs which were manned by personnel of diverse ethnic and kinship backgrounds; alienation of man in society and the attendant impersonalisation of human relations become more pronounced at the expense of gentile social and economic solidarity.

". . . what had originally been a naturally grown democracy was transformed into a hateful aristocracy. . . . the gentile constitution had grown out of a society that knew no antagonisms: But now a society had come into being that by the force of all its economic conditions of existence had to split up into freemen and slaves, into exploiting rich and exploited poor; a society that was not only incapable of reconciling these antagonisms, but had to drive them more and more to a head. Such a society could only exist either in a state of continuous, open struggle of these classes against one another or under the rule of a third power which while ostensibly standing above the classes struggling with each other, suppressed their open conflict and permitted a class struggle at most in the economic field, in a so-called legal form. The gentile constitution had outlived its usefulness. It was burst

---

[64] *Op. cit.* p. 572. Engels writes, "Here a class appears for the first time which, without taking part in production, captures the management of production as a whole and economically subjugates the producers to rule; a class that makes itself the indispensable intermediary between two producers and exploits them both. On the pretext of saving the producers the trouble and risk of exchange, of finding distant markets for their products, and of thus becoming the most useful class in society, a class of parasites arises, genuine social psychophants, who, as a reward for very insignificant real services, skin the cream off production at home and abroad, rapidly amass enormous wealth and corresponding social influence, and for this very reason are destined to reap ever new honours and gain increasing control over production during the period of civilization, until they at last create a product of their own—periodic commercial crises." *(Op. cit.,* pp. 572–73).

[65] On this development Engels writes, "Hardly had the private ownership of land been introduced when mortgage was discovered . . . . Just as Hetaerism and prostitution clung to the heels of monogamy, so from now on mortgage clung to the ownership of land." *(Op. cit.,* p. 574).

[66] *Op. cit.*

54

asunder by the division of labour and its result, the division of society into classes. Its place was taken by the state".[67]

Thus Engels regards the state not as "a power forced on society from without but rather as "a product of society at a certain stage of development".[68] Arisen out of but placing itself above society, the state, Engels argues, became necessary as an instrument of protecting the interests of the exploiting minority class in society against the wrath of the oppressed exploited mass of the people. In short, the state is nothing but public power as expressed in an armed force, gendarmerie, judiciary, tax[69] and which is used as an instrument of coercion by "the most powerful, economically dominant class, which, through the medium of the state becomes also the politically dominant class, and thus acquires new means of holding down and exploiting the oppressed class."[70]

Civilization, it is necessary to point out, is no specific socio-economic formation. It is simply, a fully developed class society with an entrenched state power. Thus, a civilization could be a feudal or slave or capitalist socio-economic formation.

The Quality of Ewe Social Set-up

We shall now attempt to identify the quality of the pre-colonial Ewe society against the background of our discussion of feudalism, AMP and Barbarism and of our claim that the AMP and Barbarism are not different in essence.

(a) Ketu

Traditional Yoruba culture is usually regarded as a high culture. Typical high culture traits are: Transition from subsistence to money economy with a developed internal and external trade; independent public enterprises such as trade and handicrafts; a hierarchically structured political organization with full-time officials, organs of coercion, such as an elaborate judiciary; decline of kinship influence and authority.[71]

Ketu city, founded by the Yoruba king Ede, was in the so-called Yoruba culture area which was known for its walled cities, developed trade and handicrafts (pottery, bronze and iron-work, weaving, leather work, etc.), subsistence agriculture, hierarchically structured administrative machinery dominated by a well-entrenched, secular aristocracy with divine undertones.

Now, the cisterns, ruined fortifications and fragments of pottery found in the Ketu province (outside the Ketu city, itself) and regarded as remnants of the Adja-Ewe culture suggests a

---

[67] *Op. cit.,* p. 575.
[68] *Op. cit,* p. 576.
[69] Engels does not (unfortunately) discuss the role of tax or the various forms of rent in the various pre-civilization modes of product'on. Though regrettable the omission might imply that Engels does not regard it (i.e. the role of rent or tribute) as a contradiction that could seriously affect the essence of the pre-civilization production relations, i.e., in terms of negation. His reference to it here may document the importance he attaches to it as a serious negative element in the period of civilization.
[70] *Op. cit.,* pp. 577-578.
[71] See Nachtigall, H. 1974, pp. 115-119.

high culture tradition of the Ketu Ewe-stock. But the high culture concept is not very useful as a tool of classification because it does not throw much light on the pattern of production relations embodied in a so-called high culture. This difficulty, not to mention the acute lack of data on the Ketu Adja-Ewe, makes it extremely difficult, if not impossible for us to classify the pre-Notsie social formation. But the material cultural skeleton briefly described above (compact villages, graves, mounds, cisterns, ruined fortifications, etc.) suggests that the Ketu Adja-Ewe had already passed the Palaeo-Communalist stage of development. And since we have argued that the Adja-Ewe culture was in the Yoruba culture area it may not be misleading to suggest that the Communalist production relations that dominated Yoruba culture in that early period constituted the essence of the Adja-Ewe mode of production in Ketu. While Ewe Oral tradition has it that land since Ketu has been communal property we are not told how the system of land possession or usufruct affected surplus distribution at Ketu; neither are we informed in detail about the super-structure at the time. In view of these difficulties we are yet unable to say exactly at what stage of Communalism they were when they migrated from Ketu.

As pointed out earlier our data on Notsie are not very helpful either; but the scanty information on the level of technological development and production relations gives us a fairly useful clue in terms of analytical deductions.

(b) Notsie Community

The Notsie political set-up was obviously a pre-capitalist non-feudal mode of production. In others words, primitive agriculture, based on the system of communal ownership of land, formed the basis of economic life. Till the slave trade, the production of use-value, that is to say, the socio-biological reproduction of the individual in well-defined relationships to his community, was the main objective behind economic activity. The mechanism of this reproduction was only possible by the individual's right of usufruct in terms of land which in turn was rooted in his membership of the community. The socio-economic reproduction of the individual in the Notsie community was thus inseparable from the unity of the community and land. The objective conditions of labour, among them land as an inorganic extension of the individuals of the community and therefore of the community as a whole, were regarded by the individual as his own and as Marx would put it, "the inorganic nature of his subjectivity, which realises itself through them".

Though the nuclear family was generally the production and consumption unit, part of the surplus labour of every production unit belonged to the community in the form of tribute and communal labour for the glory of the community whose power was embodied in the central administrative machinery headed by the king. The ability of the community to defray its costs for war,

56

for periodic festive occasions, religious rites, etc. and to ensure internal security, law and order, all constituted the glory of the community. In other words, there existed, in the Notsie political set-up, a full-time administrative nobility (and therefore the separation of mental labour from physical labour) who appropriated part of the surplus labour in return for their administrative services to the community.

The author is inclined to link the exodus from Notsie with some major contradictions which developed, as a result of the slave trade, in the mechanism of surplus appropriation by the administrative aristocracy.

As has been pointed out above, Notsie had an early access to the sea and traded with Europeans in goods and slaves.

The most serious consequence of the slave trade was the stagnation of the productive forces in pre-colonial Africa. The goods (guns, gun-powder, cheap textiles, worthless items exchanged for human labour force) were not capital goods or assets. They were mainly consumed and squandered by the ruling aristocracies, who in course of the slave trade, became addicted to consumption orgies of the most repugnant nature. Describing a royal reception he gave to the king of Warri, King Pepple, an obstinate Niger Delta ruler and slave trader, boasts in Pidgin English as follows: "That time I first hear Warri's canoe come for creek, I fire one gun from my house—then all Bonny fire—plenty powder blow away you no can hear one man speak, I stand for my house— all my house have fine cloth. Roof, walls, all round, be hung with proper fine silks. No possible to look one stick, one mat: all be covered.

"Queen Father stand for beach. His foot no touch ground. He stand on cloth...I give Wine, Brandy, plenty puncheon — pass twenty. I give for my people and Warri's, All Bonny glad too much...
"Every man, every woman, for my town, I give cloth — pass one thousand piece I give that day. Pass twenty barrel powder, I fire that day."[72]

Like in other polities on the Guinea Coast almost all commercial contacts and transactions between Notsie and European traders were channelled through the Notsie central administrative machinery. Notsie's external trade was thus controlled, if not monopolized, by the king. Since the commodities they exchanged for the European goods must be acquired or produced internally the Notsie aristocracy had to control aspects of the internal trade to ensure regularity in terms of supply in its commercial transactions with the Europeans. The regular supply of specific indigenous goods and slaves and the fixing of prices for all traded goods must have therefore been aspects of the internal trade the ruling aristocracy controlled. Because of the low development level of the forces of production in Notsie at the time, not to mention the stagnant effect of the slave trade on the economy as a whole, the

72 Davidson, B., 1966, pp. 235–236.

institutionalized regular supply of slaves and the general price control of goods meant a heavy drain on the surplus labour of the population. To be able to acquire slaves the aristocracy must have guns and gun-powder; to be able to get these foreign means of destruction there must be money or indigenous goods for exchange with the former. The source of supply of these indigenous goods was the Notsie population which could only acquire or produce the goods by working more than the necessary labour time during which the use-value of the nutritional and non-nutritional items basic to the people's simple biological and social reproduction was produced. The intensity of the surplus labour provided in the extra labour time as well as the length of the latter could only be maintained if the development of the forces of production in Notsie was always commensurate with the ever-mounting pressure by the aristocracy on the population to produce and acquire more goods and slaves for exchange. But as indicated above, the slave trade resulted in the forces of production stagnating since the relatively cheap goods received by the Africans in return for their slaves were in most cases no instruments of production.

New food plants such as maize, cassava, tomato, which could have boosted the development of the forces of production, i.e. if their production would not make the Notsie nobility increase disproportionally the volume of their surplus appropriation, could scarcely be lucratively cultivated because the Notsie environment (the Central Plains) was not particularly favourable to their growth and the crops were new and the Notsie Ewe might have needed time to get used to them.[73]

The rulers of Notsie were apparently unconscious of the contradiction between their greedy demand for slaves and other goods and the stagnating nature of the productive forces within their economic set-up. The result was an ever-increasing encroachment on the surplus labour of the population especially during the reign of Agokoli I. It may not be completely ruled out that the decision of the Notsie Ewe to migrate was taken at a time when almost the whole surplus labour of the population was appropriated by the aristocracy in the form of communal labour,[74] slave raids, tributes in money and kind, under-invoicing of internally produced commodities with the balance flowing into the coffers of the nobility. We are inclined to suggest that the socially necessary labour of the community on which their minimum biological and socio-cultural reproduction hinged, had been already encroached upon or at least seriously threatened.[75]

Hunters of feudalism in Africa would depict the Notsie social set-up, as well as post-Notsie Ewe society as a feudal formation just

[73] In fact they started cultivating these crops only after their exodus from Notsie.

[74] Building and renovation of the city walls; the erection of the houses of the nobility; construction of roads and of other public places for festive and other occasions constituted communal labour in Notsie. Informants told the author that the people of Notsie had detested one particular type of communal labour namely, drawing water several kilometers away from the city.

[75] Leklebi oral tradition still cites starvation on the eve of the rebellion as one of the main reasons for the exodus. (See Wiegrabe, P. (ed.), 1963 p. 23).

because of the partial surplus labour appropriated by the ruling aristocracy. The partial appropriation of surplus labour in the form of tribute, communal labour, war and fines by the ruling upper stratum of a pre-class society is enough evidence to categorise such a society as feudal. This erroneous position is dictated by their failure to objectively relate the essence of surplus appropriation to that of other categories of production relations in the pre-class society. As pointed out earlier, membership of the Notsie polity pre-supposed the possession of land; as a member of the social set-up, the individual production unit (could be a nuclear or extended family was a private possessor; while each production unit related to his plot of land it was aware of its being a constituent part of the community. The production unit accordingly never regarded its sustenance as divorced from the sustenance of the community. In other words, the community was the pre-supposition of the institutionalised usufruct, a pre-supposition identical with "the relation of the working subject to the natural presuppositions of labour as belonging to him". This phenomenon was compatible with the level of labour productivity which was barely above the subsistence level. Thus the survival of Notsie was rooted in "the preservation of equality among its free self-sustaining peasants, and their own labour as the condition of the survival of their property". The conditions of labour to which the Notsie peasants related were real personality building elements by means of free personal labour. Examining the relationship between property relations and surplus appropriation in ancient classical communities, Marx draws the following conclusion which excellently describes the Notsie situation: "The individual is placed in such conditions of earning his living as to make not the acquiring of wealth his object, but self-sustenance, his own reproduction as a member of the community. The survival of the commune is the reproduction of all its members as self-sustaining peasants, whose surplus time belongs precisely to the commune, the work of war, etc. The property in one's own labour is mediated by property in the condition of labour — the hide of land, guaranteed in its turn by the existence of the commune, and that in turn by surplus labour in the form of military service, etc. by the commune members. It is not co-operation in wealth — producing labour by means of which the commune member reproduces himself, but rather co-operation in labour for the communal interests (imaginary and real) for the upholding of the association inwardly and outwardly".[76]

Till the exodus, Agokoli did not in any way interfere with the traditional system of land tenure. It is not clear how all the appropriated surplus was utilized. Part of it, as pointed out earlier, was allocated for the maintenance of the royal household, while another part took the form of communal labour and wars. While we are unable to quantify the remaining part of the surplus that went to the royal house one wonders if it was significant in relation to what went back to the community as a whole. In other words,

[76] Marx, K., 1977, "Grundrisse" p. 476.

59

surplus labour was apparently at this stage not meant to produce wealth exclusively for the ruling aristocracy; it was still basically "co-operation in labour" for the protection and glorification of the community and for the sustenance and reproduction of the ruling aristocracy.[77]

This assertion does not in any way contradict our earlier suggestion that the exodus from Notsie might have been caused by the threat Agokoli I's demand for more surplus posed to the socially necessary labour of the people of Notsie. The point we are trying to stress is that the extracted surplus labour (embodied in tributes, in kind, under-invoiced goods internally produced, slave raids, communal labour)[78] was a liability rather than an asset in terms of economic growth and the development of the forces of production.[79] In fact, we have suggested that Akogoli's involvement in the slave trade gave rise to economic stagnation and that the exodus became necessary as a result of his demand for more surplus labour in spite of this development.

It would, however, be interesting to know how the European commercial items exchanged for slaves were distributed.

The riotous expensive way of life of African kings and chiefs mentioned above is an example of a general situation. Particular situations may differ from the general pattern. In fact, during our field and documentary investigations we have not come across any facts that suggest that the Notsie kings, including Agokoli I, lived in affluence or were addicted to frivolous or dissolute pleasures. Even insinuations to that effect have not come our way.

What was against this economic background, the development level of public power and authority?

We have agreed that in spite of the slave trade and other forms of commercial activity in Notsie, production of use-value still constituted the basis of the community's reproduction. This implies that the level of surplus production was not high enough to accelerate the development of social division of labour (which was at its rudimentary stage) with the attendant rapid expansion of trade, urbanization, and social stratification. Thus kinship still remained the framework of demographic and political structure. The council of lineage elders, presided over by the divine king, was accordingly the permanent political authority. Political power was therefore ultimately wielded by the whole community since the lineage heads embodied the will of the people, i.e. the free peasants. The existence of a hereditary executive council and the standing army which protected it, though might have created the opportunity for strengthening the aristocratic element, could not separate public authority from the people because of the

---

[77] We are unable because of lack of data, to relate the quantity and quality of the surplus that went to the royal household to the effectiveness and intensity of the administrative labour provided by the ruling nobility. It is therefore not possible to define exactly the degree of exploitation of the producers by those who wielded political power.
[78] Building and repairing of the city walls and roads.
[79] This development adversely affected the reproduction mechanism of the community since the greater part of the total surplus was not reproductive

60

scanty surplus produced and because every adult male member of the community was a warrior.

Even during Agokoli's tyrannical rule, this primitive democratic framework remained essentially unchanged though the separation of public power and authority from the people set in gradually as a result of multiplying contradictions which emerged in the relations of production. The growing independence of Agokoli and his executive council, backed by full-time warriors (apparently better armed and trained than other non-professional male warriors), of the elders' council and therefore of the people, was caused by the king's inability to identify and remove the chronic contradiction between the volume of appropriated surplus labour of the community and the low stagnant level of the community's productive forces.

Though this process of alienation entailed, to some extent, the brutalization of the community (including the lineage heads) by the executive aristocracy, the organs used in this exercise could not develop into full state power, neither could new organs of coercion and repression à la state emerge because of the absence of antagonistic social classes whose development was fettered by stagnation in production.

These socio-economic relations of Notsie suggest meso-communalist stage of cultural development. We are reminded of the following meso-communalist traits: The entrenched agricultural economy; fairly developed handicraft and internal trade made possible by modest surplus production in agriculture; the parallel rudimentary development of social division of labour; land as tribal property with economic units usually consanguineally structured, having right of possession; recognition of production units as consumption units in spite of legalised limited surplus appropriation by the administrative aristocracy; visible differences in the accumulated wealth of the production and consumption units organised on family-basis; the involvement of the standing army in slave raids and the subsequent increase in the aristocracy's appropriation of the people's labour; the king's monopolisation of external trade, his tight control over internal trade; the apparent utilization of part of the royal commercial gains not in the common interest of the whole community; exploitation of slave labour; despotic divine kingship backed by a professionally organized group of warriors; separation of central administrative labour from physical labour; a well-established kinship system with marked social and economic solidarity; a non-codified primitive law organically interwoven with religious, normative and ethical sanctions and mores, etc.

We have earlier posited that the exodus from Notsie might have been prompted by King Agokoli's appropriation of a substantial part of the surplus labour of his subjects and by the latter's fear that the taboos-surrounded king would encroach eventually upon their necessary labour so fundamental to their reproduction.[80]

What would happen if the exodus had not taken place is anybody's guess.

The communalist Notsie social formation could develop into a slave society should Agokoli eventually substitute slave labour for the free peasant labour which formed the basis of production by throwing some of his slaves into production and enslaving the total labour of his own subjects.

Another alternative would have been for the divine king to seize and distribute all land, on private ownership basis, among the most senior kinship heads and his top military officers who would in turn enserf the free peasants of Notsie and pay tributes as vassals to the king. These measures would substitute feudal production relations for the communalist social order.[81]

It might have also not been completely ruled out that organized resistance by the people could prevent Agokoli from resorting to any unpopular measures that might negate the meso-communalist quality of Notsie.

The Post-Notsie Society

We shall now attempt an assessment of the post-Notsie socio-economic system.

Though we have been unable, due to lack of adequate data, to quantify the volume of production and accurately assess the level of labour productivity of the Ewe in the Notsie period, we can safely assert that the post-Notsie economy was more complex in terms of structure, production and wealth distribution. The heterogeneous nature of the geographical environment of the new habitat (south Togo and south-eastern Ghana); new cultural and commercial contacts with the outside world, to be precise, with European, Akan and other African traders, and missionaries; the acquisition of new exotic food and cash crops, such as maize, manioc, tomato, cotton, coffee, etc. were all factors which favoured the development of a more complex, dynamic, economic activity. Thus, within a relatively short span of time after the Notsie exodus, labour productivity could be raised and a significant surplus produced for exchange. As pointed out in Part II specialization, e.g. in fishing, onion cultivation, salt industry, trade and handicrafts was wide-spread especially in the coastal areas. Villages soon developed into important commercial centres from where new cultural values and norms radiated to other areas of Ewe-land. Denu, Anexo, Keta, Lome, Ho, Kpando and Dukradza were already famous for their markets and for a class of professional traders who circulated commodities between country and town.

The rather lively post-Notsie economic activity thus added new dimensions to social division of labour. As indicated in Part II, semi-regional and village-ward specialization in handicrafts was also

---

[80] See Part II, Political Structure.
[81] This latter alternative could have preceded the exodus if Agokoli's elders had been loyal to him. According to Wiegrabe, the elders, who were heads of the various politico-kinship units of the Notsie polity were bitterly opposed to Agokoli's administration.

observed. Clear distinctions between town and country were a new development in certain areas, though the rural areas still exercised economic supremacy over the commercial centres.

Our examination of the post-Notsie economy reveals contradictions between the forces and relations of production; there were quantitative and qualitative differences in the wealth of families and individuals made possible by (1) unjust distribution of environmental resources vital to production; (2) different historical factors; (3) non-identity of patterns of production experience; (4) unequal marketing possibilities; and (5) the private appropriation of products in agriculture, in the salt and crafts industries, in the fishing economy, trade and animal husbandry.

Thus because of better environmental conditions the onion cultivator of the Anlo Peninsular at the coast and yam grower in the mountainous areas of the hinterland did materially better than the peasants of the drought-plagued Central Plains. The peculiar nature of the coastal strip boosted economic activity more rapidly than in the hinterland. We have in mind contacts the coastal Ewe had with European traders and the attendant exchange of ideas, which favoured the introduction of fairly large scale new economic ventures like fishing, onion and coconut cultivation in the area.

Thus there were clear material distinctions between regions. But even within one and the same region unequal distribution of environmental factors and the nature of their exploitation or use engendered material and social differentiation. Take the large stretches of coconut plantations at the coast, for instance. Some of the plots of land used were nominally property of the whole community and are still regarded by all (including those members of the community who did not own coconut plantations) as property of the community. But the coconut trees were exclusively the property of the plantation owners and no percentage of the cash income derived was given the community as rent. Thus the land, property of the community, was used by a few individuals of the community as a means of surplus appropriation at the expense of the community whether or not alien labour, including that of community members, was exploited.

Thus while the land was nominally communal property, in practice, it was privately owned. This praxis was temporally "diachronized" by the right of inheritance over the coconut plantations.

Similar developments were taking place in the salt and lagoon-fishing industries. The first-come-first-served principle in the salt industry, though recognised only seasonally, could serve as a means of individual wealth accumulation, especially, if the same people or a high percentage of them succeeded in capturing salt grounds uninterrupted several seasons at the expense of others.

The anti-democratic element in the "Abla" method of lagoon-fishing was the right to inherit the *xadowo*. It is obvious that the praxis was direct privatization of rich fishing grounds of the collectively owned lagoon. Right of inheritance here suggests that the demand for rich fishing grounds in the lagoon exceeded what was available.

63

Sea-fishing was not exploitation-free either. The 50 per cent of the catches that went to the net-owner and the 25 per cent claimed by the boat-owner smacks of exploitation.

The privileged coconut plantation owners and their counterparts in the salt and lagoon-fishing industries did not put at the disposal of the community part of their surpluses as rent.

These privileges did not only constitute means of material differentiation in the pre-colonial time; they have also served as sources of capital formation for families and individuals since the colonial era.

The emergence of professional traders, caused by high labour productivity, was a new non-gentile feature in the post-Notsie economic activity. The professional nature of commercial activity is proof that the traders were feeding on the surplus they extracted from producers and consumers of the commodities they marketed. We are again here reminded, among others, of the 100 German-mark profit coastal traders made on every slave child in the last days of the slave trade.

The appropriation of the surplus labour of slaves and bondsmen was a very important symptom of class distinction.

Both the exploiter and the exploited among the commoners paid some tributes to the nobility of the Du. As observed in Part II of this essay, specific parts of leopard, lion or elephant killed, as well as a certain quantity of merchandised goods, meat and other foodstuffs, court fees, free seasonal labour were the main types of tribute paid by the commoners, besides regular communal labour and occasional military operations. Unfortunately we lack information on how war booties were disposed of. But that a certain percentage went to the nobility could scarcely be disputed.

The post-Notsie super-structure as outlined in Part II still maintained old Notsie features, such as kinship structure, hierarchically structured political power wielded by firmly established nobilities who ruled through administrative and executive councils; non-codified, but well-defined legal system, moral and normatic santions, religious ideas and taboos, nascent social stratification, etc.

Influenced by the new economic relations and historical factors some of these super-structural features assumed new structural and functional dimensions in the post-Notsie period. For example, gradual transition to private ownership of means of production and products intensified the division of the members of a kinship unit, of a village into rich and poor, thereby changing rapidly the community of social economic solidarity into antagonism between members of one and the same consanguineal unit. Expansion of trade gave rise to gradual urbanization (in commercially strategic and active centres) and the attendant systematic disintegration of kinship-based demographic structures; and anonymity, coupled with impersonalisation of human relations. The favourable heterogeneous environmental conditions in the new habitat, instrumental in the fairly rapid development of economic activity, encouraged the distribution of the population over wide areas, a factor which played no mean role in the decentralisation of political power and authority.

The decentralisation of political power, and the subsequent involvement of wider circles of the population in local administration and decision-making stopped the dangerous trend of separation of executive and military power from the people which had set in at Notsie under Agokoli I.

War was not only waged to avenge aggression or expand territory, but it was also waged "for the sake of plunder". However, kinship still remained the structural basis of military organisation. The fighting forces (comprising every able-bodied male member of a Du) did not therefore constitute at this stage an alienated organ of coercion totally separated from the people. The repressive nature of their domestic functions revealed itself, however, in the protection the military institutions gave to the growing contradictions in the post-Notsie production relations.

The loss of central political authority and full-time administration in favour of a more liberal system of power dissemination did not therefore in any way prevent the development of rudimentary class antagonisms within the new political frame-work. Property law was modified, to a limited degree, to protect the right to privately own important means of production. The process of social stratification was accelerated by new economic events, with the law recognising and protecting the right of the nobility and rich individuals to usurp the surplus labour of slaves and bondsmen, while the class of traders could freely exploit consumers and direct producers.

As in Notsie, Religion was still a powerful instrument of socio-economic and political control, which was exploited, not only by the ruling aristocracies and the priesthood, but also by individual rich men, medicine men and by newly emerged pressure institutions, such as the Yewe and Wudu Secret societies.

These new repressive super-structural traits were just like the new economic contradictions still undeveloped. In other words, the gentile socio-economic quality still dominated post-Notsie Ewe society.

We may support this proposition with the following arguments:

1. Like in Notsie the production of use-value based mainly on agriculture still permeated economic activity. The post-Notsie society, was sustained by communal ownership of usufructuary status of land. In other words, though known and practised the production of exchange value was marginal while membership of the post-Notsie society, like in Notsie society, was sustained by communal ownership land. Land, the decisive objective condition of labour, was therefore regarded as sacred and under normal circumstances not saleable. Even in one or two rare cases where plots of land were privatised through sale the private status of the land concerned assumed again possessory title after

65

a generation or two because of the intactness of the society's kinship structural and functional framework.

2. The identified cheating praxis in the coconut, salt and fishing industries where individuals or families for a long time used parts of the communally owned land and lagoon not only to earn their living but also to acquire wealth at the expense of the community was spatially restricted. In addition, in most cases personal or family labour was involved. And though the surplus acquired through the cheating was clearly an advantage infrastructural and marketing constraints at the time might have considerably contained its contribution to rapid social stratification and decline of the communalist social order.

3. The survival of the post-Notsie society was identical with the reproduction of most of its members as free self-sustaining peasants. In other words, free peasant labour was the dominant labour pattern that sustained the society in spite of the exploitation of the labour of slaves and bondsmen here and there.

4. While the appropriation of the surplus labour of the free common people by one or two chiefs,' especially in the coastal areas, smacks of exploitation, in most cases, however, the people's surplus labour in form of tributes, military service, communal work, etc. guaranteed the existence and sovereignty of the society. Like in Notsie it was co-operation in labour for the communal interest, identity and protection.

5. Kinship still remained the basis of demographic and political structure even in the emerging urban communities. The nobility, that is the *Fiahawo* and *Dumegãwo*, representing the various kinship units (and presided over by the chief) was, therefore, the ultimate political authority, which in turn, was embedded in the power of the common people.

But since membership of these Councils was by descent and therefore anti-democratic, there was room for public authority getting eventually separated from the people. This possible development was, however, contained at the time by the gentile democratic content of the military apparatus (where every able-bodied male was warrior) and the institution of *Sohewo*, super- structural institutions which were still effective because of the rather low level of production of exchange value.

In the final analysis, however, the above arguments do not negate the fact that generally, the post-Notsie socio-economic contradictions and modifications were actively paving the way for the full development of social classes and the attendant state power. In fact, we could dare propose that they had already pushed the Ewe into late communalism (i.e. Morgan/Engels' Upper Barbarism)

66

before the first Christian missionaries arrived in south-eastern Ghana and Togo in the 20s of the 19th century.

b The chart below is an attempt to highlight again the identical qualities of the Asiatic Mode of Production, Barbarism and Pre-colonial Ewe communalist society. In spite of the indication of external properties our emphasis is on the essence of production relations as the decisive classification criterion.

Conclusion

The ancestors of the Ewe, just like those of any other ethnic groups elsewhere, certainly went through a Paleo-Communalist, (i.e. Morgan/Engels' Savage) Stage of cultural development. We have been unable, due to lack of data, to deal with the Paleo-Communalist past of the Ewe. Our attempt to dive into Ewe life in Ketu has yielded only scanty results, again because of lack of information. We have cautiously concluded from the limited information, both documentary and oral, at our disposal, that the Ketu Ewe had possibly attained a communalist stage of development, a level they maintained till their migration to Notsie. It has been impossible to identify the exact stage of communalism they had.

We have posited that Notsie society was a Meso-Communalism formation, and that on the eve of the exodus Late Communalist features became more pronounced.

We have then concluded from our analysis of the post-Notsie socio-economic set-up that the Ewe reached, but still remained at the Late stage of Communalism till formal colonization in spite of the fairly rapid development of their forces of production.

The State, as an apparatus of repression, was never fully developed among the Ewe. Though still at its rudimentary stage of development, it showed characteristics of repression here and there, a phenomenon which reflected the gradual development of tensions between the forces and relations of production as time went on.

I am not making claim to great merits as far as the general conclusions in this essay are concerned. My position is a simple one, namely, (1) that the Ewe society has never been a feudal, but rather communalist mode of production; (2) that all traditional societies, whether African or not, whose production relations are qualitatively identical with those of the pre-colonial Ewe cannot be anything other than communalist formations; (3) that the Asiatic Mode of Production is essentially barbarism" and therefore communalist.

6

Asiatic Mode of Production (Equivalent to Barbarism)
Economic Relations

Economy: Subsistence agriculture with modest surplus production—however, agriculture is not the only type of economy that could form the sub-base of an AMP formation; handicrafts and undeveloped internal and external trade; division of labour by sex co-existing with a rudimentary social division of labour—especially between agriculture and handicraft; free peasant labour as basis of production and reproduction, co-existing with slave labour.

Property Relations

Private ownership of personal tools and weapons; common ownership of land (as the most important means of production) with each community member enjoying the right of possession; communality of labour, or the nuclear or extended family as production and consumption unit; surplus

Barbarism
Economic Relations

Lower Barbarism — Economy

Cultivation of edible plants or pastoralism as a self-sufficient undertaking or a combination of hunting, fishing and subsistence agriculture; undeveloped intra-tribal and inter-tribal trade; dominance of division of labour by sex; rudimentary development of specialised handicraft. Scanty surplus product; free peasant labour as basis of production and reproduction.

Production Relations

Private ownership of personal tools and weapons, common ownership of land and grazing grounds; collectively produced items as common property; gradual conversion of herds into separate property; prevalence of harmony between the forces and relations of productions.

Pre-Colonial Ewe Society
Economic Relations

Ketu Period (Communalism — exact stage not known)

Economy: Complex subsistence economy — agriculture, handicraft and hunting; possible exchange based on use-value; possible use of iron tools; low level of productivity because of environmental hostility (drought and bad soil); division of labour by sex; semi-social division of labour; free peasant labour possibly the basis of production.

Production Relations

Communal ownership of land; production units no doubt as consumption units; possible partial appropriation of surplus labour by the ruling nobility, a praxis probably too insignificant to disrupt the harmony between forces and relations of production.

Asiatic Mode of Production
(Equivalent to Barbarism)
Economic Relations

labour — expressed in communal works and tributes appropriated by the community partly for the maintenance of the administrative nobility and the priesthood and partly as common community funds. Social economic solidarity; relative harmony between the productive forces and production relations.

Barbarism
Economic Relations

Middle Barbarism — Economy

Mixed complex economy (agriculture, handicraft, livestock breeding), though pastoralism still here and there as a separate undertaking; use and working up of metals (iron, copper, tin, bronze, gold and silver), technique of weaving loom; increase in production; exploitation of slave labour; free peasant labour as basis of production.

Production Relations

Land as tribal property with community members enjoying the right of possession; conversion of herds into individual property; production units as consumption units; partial appropriation of the community's surplus labour in the form of tributes and public works by the ruling aristocracy for the reproduction of the latter and for common public good.

Pre-colonial Ewe Society
Economic Relations
Notsie Period (Meso-Communalism)

Economy: Before the Slave Trade essentially like that of Ketu; however higher labour productivity because of more favourable environment and addition of rice to old cereals. During the slave trade — increase in production and higher labour productivity; gradual separation of handicrafts from agriculture; active internal and external trade with slaves as most important commodity; money as medium of exchange; free peasant labour as basis of production; separation of administrative labour from physical labour — determined partially by taboo.

Production relations as in Ketu; however intensified surplus appropriation by the community.

69

Asiatic Mode of Production (Equivalent to Barbarism) Economic Relations	Barbarism Economic Relations	Pre-colonial Ewe Society Economic Relations
	Upper Barbarism — Economy	**Post-Notsie Period (Late Communalism)**
	Further development of the forces of production, dominance of iron implements and weapons; walled towns with inclosing stone houses; rapid increase in wealth due to high level of labour productivity; intensification of social division of labour culminating in the separation of handicrafts from agriculture; cultivation of more edible plants in addition to the already-known cereals; appearance of commodity production and expansion of internal trade; development of money; exploitation of slave labour intensified; free peasant labour constituting the basis of production.	Economy: Complex economy: subsistence agriculture; appearance of cash crop economy (rubber, cotton and coconut plantations), acquisition of new foreign crops; fishing, hunting, handicrafts, internal and external trade; money as medium of exchange; salt industry. Intensification of social division of labour, specialisation in production; development of commercial centres into towns; in short rapid development of the forces of production made possible by very favourable environmental conditions and historical factors; free labour dominating production.
	Production Relations	*Production Relations*
	Gradual accomplishment of the transition to complete private ownership of land; individual family becoming the economic	Communal ownership of land despite sporadic private acquisition of land here and there; insignificant payment of tributes in money, in kind and labour; exploitation of slave labour and

Asiatic Mode of Production
(Equivalent to Barbarism)
Economic Relations

Barbarism
Economic Relations

unit in society; disintegration of kinship household communities due to differences in the wealth of family heads; Productive Forces — Productive Relations relationships assuming more antagonistic nature due to the conversion of important means of production (land inclusive) into private property; exaction of taxes and tributes by the administrative machinery, communal labour for the glorification of the community as a whole; appropriation of slave labour.

of bondsmen (however not widespread); gradual distinction between town and country; production units as consumption units with the nuclear family dominantly becoming the economic unit in society; appropriation of surplus products by professional and semi-professional traders; differences in the wealth of families and individuals more pronounced; private acquisition of different categories of means of production; thus marked but undeveloped contradictions between the forces and relations of production.

Asiatic Mode of Production
(Equivalent to Barbarism)
Super-structure

Central administration, either on village or tribal level — however an Asiatic Mode of Production could also have an acephalous political organization.

Well-developed kinship system whose sub-units are at the same time the units of the political structure; executive and administrative machinery mainly manned by an embryonic nobility; priestly aristocracy; religion as a means of spiritual reinforcement and social control; organized military power; non-codified, but well-defined law; rudimentary development of class antagonisms (e.g. slave labour and possible unjust partial appropriation of the community's surplus labour by the secular and priestly aristocracies); personal human relations; dominance of popular assembly, equality in privileges and rights protected by democratic gentile constitution.

Barbarism
Super-structure

Lower Barbarism

Fully developed kinship system; the tribe as the highest, largest kinship and political unit; a confederacy of kin tribes here and there; absence of social classes; elders' councils; popular assembly, vendetta; war as a means of settling conflicts and not a means of subjugation; personal human relations; social and economic solidarity; equality in privileges and personal rights; liberty, equality, fraternity as cardinal principles protected by gentile organs of social control.

Middle Barbarism

Super-structure here essentially identical with that of Lower Barbarism; however gradual development of social stratification based on the exploitation of slave labour and more surplus production; the subsequent development of private property law, organs

Pre-colonial Ewe Society
Super-structure

Ketu Period (Communism—Stage not known)

Fully developed kinship system; a ruling aristocracy; primitive organs of administration, such as elders' councils, chiefs' executive councils, armed warriors, legal, moral and religious sanctions, popular assembly. Possible equality in rights and privileges; possible rudimentary development of social classes.

Notsie Period (Meso-Communalism)

Rigid centralized authority embodied in a divine, absolute ruler; powerful administrative and executive councils; professional warriors; a well-defined legal system with religious under-tones; rudimentary social stratification based on differences in wealth accumulation; partial suppression of personal freedom and brutalisation of the people by the aristocracy (but only in Agokoli's era); kinship structure still entrenched.

| **Asiatic Mode of Production** (Equivalent to Barbarism) Super-structure | Super-structure | *Pre-Colonial Ewe Society* Super-structure |

Post-Notsie Period (Late Communalism)

Decentralised political authority wielded by local nobilities; organs of social control—elders' councils, chiefs' administrative and executive councils, legal system with new features, organized, but not professional warriors; pressure groups (recognised opposition groups, secret societies); gradual appearance of social classes (slaves, bondsmen, traders, craftsmen). Kinship system still intact.

Super-structure

of social control still essentially democratic though used as a means of protecting emerging social and material privileges and oppressing slaves and bondsmen.

Upper Barbarism

Kinship system still in tact, though structurally and functionally weakened through the concentration of more power in the hands of military leaders and the nobility and intensification of social stratification generated by growing property differences between kinship groups and individuals. Further development of classes, especially the class of slaves and merchants in spite of the fact that free peasant labour still constituted the basis of production. Growing economic and political power of the ruling aristocracy; gradual impersonalization of human relations especially in the newly emerging towns; further development of

Asiatic Mode of Production
(Equivalent to Barbarism)
Super-Structure

Super-Structure

property law; wars of plunder and subjugation; organs of coercion (legal system, executive and administrative councils, military institution — now becoming professional) become more repressive and gradually assume state features.

Pre-colonial Ewe Society
Super-Structure

74

APPENDIX

D.K.Bl	—	Deutsches Kolonial-blatt
D.K.Z	—	Deutsche Kolonial-zeitung
M E W	—	Mark/Engels-Werke
Wiss. Zeitsch	—	Wissenschaftliche Zeitschrift
Ztf. f. Ethnol.	—	Zeitschrift fuer Ethnologie
M. a.d. sch.	—	Mitteilungen aus den Deutschen Schutzgebieten

BIBLIOGRAPHY

Amenumey, D.,
"The Problem of Dating the Accession of the Ewe People to their present Habitat". In: *Proceedings of the conference on Yoruba Civilization,* Ife (ed. I. E. Akinjogbin and G. O. Ekemode) 1978, pp. 133–153.

Akinjogbin, I.,
The Expansion of Oyo and the Rise of Dahomey 1600–1800 in History of West Africa Vol. I, (ed. by Ajayi and Crowder), London, 1971.

Akoli, F.,
Notsie alo miafe Dzofe. In: *Ewegbegbalexexle Vol. IV,* Accra, 1963 (ed. by P. Wiegrabe).

Asamoa, A.,
Die gesellschaftlichen Verhaeltnisse der Ewe—Bevoelkerung in Suedost— Ghana, Berlin, 1971.

—*Die oekonomischen Grundlagen der verschiedenen traditionellen Autoritaetsformen in Ghana,* Leipzig, 1964 (unpublished Masters thesis).

Boahen, A.,
Topics in West African History, London, 1966.

Boateng, H.,
A Geography of Ghana, Cambridge, 1959.

Canstatt, D.,
Die gewerblichen Erzeugnisse des Togogebiets in D. K. Z., Berlin 1900, Jg. 17, Nr. 48 (N.F.13 Jg.) S 551 ff.

Chesneaux, J.,
Le Mode de Production Asiatique. In: *Editions Sociales,* Parts, 1969, pp. 13–45.

Davidson, B.,
Vom Sklavenhandel zur Kolonialisierung, Reinbek b/Hamburg, 1966.
Der Baumwollbau in Togo. In: *D. K.-Bl.,* Berlin 1911, Jg. 22, Nr. 6, S. 299–33,

Dobb, M.,
Entwicklung des Kapitalismus, Koeln/Berlin 1972.

Engels, F.,
Anti-Duehring, Moscow 1969.

—*The Origin of the Family, Private Property and the State* in: Marx/Engels,

Selected Works, Vol. 3, Moscow, 1973.

—*Die Markt* in: *MEW Bd: 19:* Berlin, 1962.

Fies, K.,
Der Yambau in Deutsch-Togo in: *Globus 84,* Braunschweig 1903, S. 266–71.

Godelier, M.,
La Notion de 'Mode de Production Asiatique' et les Schémas marxistes d'évolution des Societes in: *Editions sociales,* Paris, 1969, pp. 47–100:

Goldberg,
Bericht ueber die wirtshaftlischen Verhaettnisse des Togo-gebiets. In: *D.K.-BL.,* 1892, S: 168 ff:

Gibbs, L., (ed))
Peoples of Africa, New York, London, etc., 1965:

Guenther, R. and Schrot G.,
"Bemerkungen zur Gesetzmaessigkeit in der auf Sklaverei beruhenden Gesellschafts-ordning". In: Wiss Zeitsch der Karl-Marx-Universitaet, Gesellschafts-und Sprachwiss, Reihe 12, Jahrg, (1963), Heft 1 Leipzig, 1963.

Guhr, K.,
Karl Marx und Theoretische Probleme der Ethnographie, Jahrbuch des Museums fuer Voelkerkunde zu Leipzig (Beiheft) Berlin 1969.

Habermeier, K.,
Zur Theorie nichtkapitalistischer Gesellschafts-formation; das Beispiel drei staatlich zentralisierier Klassengeseuschaften, Heidelberg; 1973 (unblished M.A. thesis).

Haertter, G.,
Der Fischfang in Evheland. In: Ztf F. Ethnol: Ed. 38, Berlin, 1906, S 51 ff.

—*Einige Bousteine zur Geschichte der Evhe-Staemme.* In: Beitraege zur Kolonialpolitik und Kolonialwirtschaft, Bd.3, Berlin, 1901/02, S. 436–40.

Herold, B.,
Wirtshaftliches Leben und Eisenbahnbau in Togo. In: M.a.d. Sch., 1893 S. 266 ff.

Lange, O.,
Political Economy Vol. I,
Oxford/London/New York/Paris 1963.

Manoukian, H.,
The Ewe-speaking people of Togoland and the Gold Coast, London, 1952.

Manshard, W.,
Die Geographischen Grundlagen der Wirtschaft Ghanas, Wiesbaden, 1961.

Marx, K., and Engels, F.,
The German Ideology, Moscow, 1968.

Marx, K.,
Grundrisse.
Aylesbury, 1977.

—*Capital Vol. I–III,*
Moscow, 1971.
Morgan L.
Ancient Society.
London, 1877.

Mote, S.,
"Blemakesinotowo". In: Ewegbegbalexexle, Vol. IV, Accra, 1963, p. 63 (Wiegrabe P., ed.)

Mote, S.,
Blemasitsatsa In: Ewegbegbalexexle, Vol. IV, Accra, p.60.

Murdock, G.,
Social Structure, New York, 1960.

—*Africa, Its Peoples And Their Culture History,* New York/Toronto/London 1959.

Nachtigall, H.
Das sakrale Koeniastum bei Naturvoelkern und die Entstchung frueher Hochkulturen in: ZFE, 1958.

Nukunya, G.
Kinship and Marriage Among the Anlo Ewe, New York 1969.

Ottenberg, P.
Toronto/London, etc. 1965 (ed. James Gibbs) pp. 3–40. New York/Chicago

Parrinder, E.
Theistic Beliefs of the Yoruba and Ewe peoples of West Africa. In:
African ideas of God, London, 1950, p. 224 ff.

——*The Story of Ketu*, Ibadan, 1956.

Potechin, I.,
On Feudalism of the Ashanti (International Congress of Orientalists.)
Moscow, 1960.

Prah, K.
Essays on African Society and History, Accra, 1976.

Rattray, R.
Ashanti, London, 1923.

——*Ashanti Law and Constitution*, London, 1929.

Ryazanskaya, S. (ed.)
Marx/Engels Selected Correspondence, Moscow, 1965.

Seidel, H.
Die Ephe-Neger. In: *Globus 68*, Braunschweig, 1895, p. 313 ff.

Seidel, H.,
Handgewerbe der Evheneger in Togo. In: *D.K.Z. N.F. 15*, Jg., Berlin 1800.
Nr. 14, s. 147 ff.

Sellnow, I.
Grundprinzipien einer Periodisierung der Urgeschichte, Berlin, 1961:

Spieth J.,
Die Ewe-Staemme, Berlin, 1906.

Suret-Canale, J
*Les Societes Traditionnelles en Afrique Tropicale et le Concept de Mode
de Production Asiatique.* In: *Editions Sociales*, Paris, 1969, pp. 101–134.

Tait, D.
The Konkomba of Northern Ghana, London/Ibadan/Accra 1961,

Werder, P. von.
Sozialgefuege in Westafrika. In: *Zeitsch: f. vergl:Rechtswissenschaft*, Bd.
52. Stuttgart, 1937, H.1.

Wertheim, W.
Evolution and Revolution, (Penguin) 1974.

Westermann, D.,
Der Afrikaner heute und morgen (2nd Ed.), Leipzig/Essen/Berlin, 1937.

——*Die Glidyi-Ewe in Togo*, Berlin, 1935.

—*Geschichte Afrikas*, Koeln. 1952:

——*Voelkerbewegungen auf der Goldkueste in Westafrika* in *Beitraege zur
Gesellungs-und Voelk-erwissenschaft*, Berlin, 1950.

Wittfogel K.,
Marxismus und Wirtschaftgeschichte, Frankfurt/M, 1970.